AN ILLUSTRATED ORAL HISTORY

LaHave Bakery

The Building, *the* Baker, and *the* Recipes that Revitalized a Community

Jane Morrigan *and* Susan Ivany

NIMBUS PUBLISHING
— NIMBUS.CA —

Copyright © 2024, Jane Morrigan and Susan Ivany

All rights reserved. No part of this book may be reproduced, stored in a retrieval system or transmitted in any form or by any means without the prior written permission from the publisher, or, in the case of photocopying or other reprographic copying, permission from Access Copyright, 1 Yonge Street, Suite 1900, Toronto, Ontario M5E 1E5.

Nimbus Publishing Limited
3660 Strawberry Hill Street, Halifax, NS, B3K 5A9
(902) 455-4286 nimbus.ca

Printed and bound in Canada

NB1728
Editor: Angela Mombourquette
Cover art: © Kat Frick Miller
Cover design: Heather Bryan
Interior design: Jenn Embree
Calligraphy for cover and recipe section: Marnie Troyer

Nimbus Publishing is based in Kjipuktuk, Mi'kma'ki, the traditional territory of the Mi'kmaq People.

Library and Archives Canada Cataloguing in Publication

Title: LaHave Bakery : the building, the baker, and the recipes that revitalized a community / Jane Morrigan and Susan Ivany.
Names: Morrigan, Jane, author. | Ivany, Susan, author.
Description: "An illustrated oral history."
Identifiers: Canadiana (print) 20230597580 | Canadiana (ebook) 20230597599 | ISBN 9781774712726 (softcover) | ISBN 9781774712979 (EPUB)
Subjects: LCSH: LaHave Bakery—History. | LCSH: Bakeries—Nova Scotia—LaHave—History. | LCSH: LaHave Bakery—Anecdotes. | LCSH: Watson, Gael—Anecdotes.
Classification: LCC TX763 .M67 2024 | DDC 641.81/5—dc23

Nimbus Publishing acknowledges the financial support for its publishing activities from the Government of Canada, the Canada Council for the Arts, and from the Province of Nova Scotia. We are pleased to work in partnership with the Province of Nova Scotia to develop and promote our creative industries for the benefit of all Nova Scotians.

For Gael

and

In memory of Gloria Barrett
April 13, 1942–October 5, 2023

Praise for
LaHave Bakery: The Building, the Baker, and the Recipes that Revitalized a Community

LaHave Bakery: The Building, the Baker, and the Recipes that Revitalized a Community is a delightful read that celebrates the power of food, community, and resilience. Morrigan and Ivany have created a book that is not only informative and engaging but also deeply inspiring. Whether you are a history buff, a baking enthusiast, or someone who appreciates stories of community spirit, this book is sure to resonate with you. The accompanying website enhances the experience, offering a virtual connection to this special place. Together, the book and the website provide a comprehensive and heartwarming look at LaHave Bakery and its role in revitalizing a community.
> – *Canadiancookbooks.ca, Canadians + Food, July 8, 2024*

It was such a pleasure to immerse myself in this beautifully bound book, this treasure of history, this incredible story of how the LaHave Bakery became the "go to" destination for all things delectable and a must-stop destination for anyone traveling along Nova Scotia's South Shore!
> – *Atlantic Book Reviews, Reading and Reviewing Atlantic Canadian Books, May 8, 2024*

A meal in this country never springs from nowhere. I found a good example of this fact in *LaHave Bakery*. Told in alternating snippets by the proprietor Gael Watson and a cadre of co-workers, friends, family, and community members, this book is the charming tale of a shop on Nova Scotia's South Shore. The story of these entrepreneurial and enterprising women is more engrossing than it might at first seem, with its behind-the-scenes look at what it takes to build a successful food business in Canada. Watson's forty-year journey, from buying a dilapidated outfitter on a wharf to turning it into a lodestar bakery-cum-grocery-cum-bookshop, reads like a particularly Canadian tale, with its emphasis on civility, honesty, shopping local, and seeing potential in wackadoo ideas. The recipes don't hurt either.
> – *Literary Review of Canada, November 2024*

Table of Contents

Foreword by Gael Watson 1

Introduction 3

Voices 7

PART 1: Before the Bakery

CHAPTER 1   History of the LaHave Outfitting Company Building, 1901–1984 10

PART 2: LaHave Bakery: The Early Years

CHAPTER 2   Beginnings 26

CHAPTER 3   Open for Business 40

CHAPTER 4   Rising Above the Ordinary 54

CHAPTER 5   Extraordinary Times 64

CHAPTER 6   The Bakery Boat 76

PART 3: Momentum

CHAPTER 7   Bread 88

CHAPTER 8   More Than Bread 97

CHAPTER 9   More Than a Bakery 108

CHAPTER 10   Fair Banks Grocery 123

CHAPTER 11   Covid Times 129

CHAPTER 12   Working at the Bakery 134

CHAPTER 13   An Unconventional Business 149

PART 4: Past, Present, Future

CHAPTER 14   Glimpses into the Past 164

CHAPTER 15   LaHave Today 174

CHAPTER 16   An Eye to the Future 179

CHAPTER 17   Reflections 188

The Baker: A Poem by Gael Watson 196

PART 5: The Recipes

CHAPTER 18   *A Taste of LaHave Bakery: A Baker's Dozen* 198

Bread Recipes 200

     Helpful Bread-Making Tips 201

     Anadama Bread 202

     Cheddar Cheese and Herb Bread 204

     Milk and Honey Bread 206

     Oatmeal Molasses Honey Bread 208

     Potato Bread 210

     Raisin Orange Bread 212

     Seed Bread 214

     Cheddar Cheese Scones 216

Sweets Recipes 219

     Butter Tarts 220

     Carrot Cake 222

     Date Squares 224

     Lemon Squares 226

     Mocha Cake 228

Acknowledgements 230

Endnotes 232

Foreword

THE LAHAVE BAKERY BUILDING OWES ITS SPECIAL CHARACTER AND ITS CONTINUED existence to many people. But the whole story never would have happened without my former husband, Michael Watson, whose imagination and fire lit the fuse that gave us the audacity to purchase LaHave Outfitting Company in its wild and dramatic condition in 1984.

Every summer through the 1950s and '60s my family would pack up the car and head to Lunenburg County, travelling first in a 1948 Austin A40. My father would take out the back seat and replace it with a wooden platform piled with eiderdowns and pillows. It would be a three-day journey—and it was way more fun than Christmas.

In 1965, my parents bought a very old burned-out stone farmhouse in Elgin, Quebec. We gutted and renovated it as a family. My brother and my sisters were sixteen, fourteen, and nine years old at the time. I was twelve. I suspect our parents thought this distraction would keep us out of teenager trouble. It didn't, quite. However, we all loved "the farm" as we called it, and all of us loved the work and the house with all its mysteries. My experience of taking the farm from a mouldering shell to a solid house gave me, in 1984, confidence that LaHave Outfitters could be revived, even in its sorry state.

Through the years, my sisters Kim and Jane, who both have farms, have kept me on track as constant sources of practical knowledge in terms of the challenges of producing food. When Jane began her dairy farm in 1980 there were twelve hundred dairy farms in Nova Scotia. Now there are only two hundred, and only one that ships organic milk. Her animal welfare practices and focus on quality of life for the animals have helped me understand the value of these principles in all our lives. My sisters were farmers who showed me that a healthy environment, good food, and mental well-being are worthy goals for all animals—humans included. These values are at the core of LaHave Bakery's products and key to the lives of our employees, whose skills and commitment are so essential. I'm grateful for having the opportunity to employ so many wonderful people.

This book has been brought about solely through the efforts and energy of my sister Jane and my sister-in-law, Susan. Jane is brilliant, hands down. She has always been one to observe, question, and learn as much as she can. She has encouraged me to think and to look a little deeper into what is in my mind. It is important to her to be accurate as well as fair and honest. Susan shares these values and brings her own unique qualities and personality as well as her straightforward perspective. She can winnow out and focus a story. She is a force, and—fortunately—she has a sense of humour.

The writing process went like this: over the winter of 2021, Jane would drive from her farm in Pictou County to my house in Crousetown. We would sit in front of a good fire with a bottle of wine and a tape recorder between us. Of course, we would digress often, happily chatting the hours away. Meanwhile, at home, Susan—who did all the transcribing—spent hundreds of hours following the drift of our remembrances. That was a true labour of love! Over the next year and a half, Susan and Jane worked as a team to create the chapters of the book. After each chapter was finished, I was given the opportunity to read it over and make any changes and corrections before approving it. Given that we covered almost four decades, it was quite an exercise in chronology.

There is a reason this book is a gathering of different voices. I love to tell stories and, as I grow older, the telling changes. This created a conundrum for me when Jane suggested writing the story of the bakery. Finally, Jane called me with an idea that she and Susan had: why not ask some of the people who have shared this building, this place, these years? I was grateful for that suggestion, and what a time they have had pulling that idea off!

I love the bakery and all that it has given me: a lifetime of work, observation, trials, errors, and a deep understanding of the value of people. There is no way I could have done it alone.

And without Jane and Susan's patience and determination, this story would never have come to print. I am honoured that they prevailed.

Gael Watson
March 2024

Introduction

"When they bought it, it was nothing, it was just falling down. It was just a breath from being what you collect at the curb when the garbage truck goes by."
(GLORIA BARRETT, 2021)

THIS IS A STORY ABOUT A MARVELLOUS BAKERY THAT HAS BECOME LOVED AND famous. It is about an old building that seems to breathe a life of its own. It's about a successful small business in a rural community on the South Shore of Nova Scotia. It's about an extraordinary woman who has managed to create, maintain, and build upon an impressive complex of ventures within the three stories of the historic building that still bears the name LaHave Outfitting Co., Ltd.

The idea for a book about LaHave Bakery started back in 2007. Gael Watson, the proprietor, and I, (Jane), were keen to "write something up." Gael and I made notes and were excited at the prospect. Then life came banging at our doors; we were over-the-top busy with work and family and the idea went into hibernation until January 2021. By that time, Susan and I were retired. That's when I suggested recording interviews with Gael and others to gather oral histories as a way of documenting the story of the bakery. Knowing how much I wanted to make this book happen, Susan offered to transcribe the recorded interviews. We presented the idea to Gael, and she exclaimed, "Let's do it!"

The result is a remarkable story told through the voices of nine people, each distinctly and intimately connected to LaHave Bakery. Through their recollections, they share memories and reflections of the bakery, the building, and the community.

Gael Watson, the primary voice, along with her adult children, friends, and employees past and present, were interviewed during the winter of 2021. I (Jane) made many trips to the South Shore to tape-record their stories and experiences. Winter evenings with Gael, both of us nursing glasses of wine while sitting in front of an open fire, were filled with stops and starts and an animated flood of facts and stories, told in Gael's distinctive, thoughtful way. I also spent many additional hours over that winter visiting and interviewing Gloria Barrett, Kathryn Gordon, Peggy Greer, Bev Kaulback, Laura Pitts, Jesse Watson, Sadie Watson, and Andra White. While I carried out these interviews, Susan worked away, determinedly transcribing each interview.

From the transcripts, we identified themes, common threads, unique stories, revelations, and multigenerational insights. The structure for the book emerged and took shape. Excerpts were selected and the voices came to life on paper.

We hope that you, the reader, will enjoy these voices as they inform, entertain, and inspire with their stories of tenacity, ingenuity, and opportunity through the many moments and events connected to their experience of the bakery. Our intention with *LaHave Bakery: The Building, the Baker, and the Recipes that Revitalized a Community* is to illuminate the growth and success of the business as it progressed from strive, to survive, to flourish. Examples of the principles and practices that stem from Gael's unique way of doing business— what I affectionately call "Gael's School of Economics"—permeate the story. Also threaded throughout are testaments to Gael's sustained commitment to producing delicious, nutritious, locally sourced, wholesome foods.

The book begins with the history of the LaHave Outfitting Company building, whose name has become synonymous with the LaHave Bakery, beginning with its construction in 1901 as a ship chandler and general store. We also examine other enterprises, independent of the bakery, that are housed in the building, such as the LaHave Craft Co-op, Homegrown Skateboards, and LaHave River Books. Included in this book are images, some dating from the building's early days at the turn of the twentieth century, others encompassing the bakery's beginnings in 1984 up to the present day. Also featured are selected recipes for popular LaHave Bakery breads and sweets.

This is a story that has been waiting to be written. Gael Watson has been approached over the years by a number of writers wishing to do just that. Because of our personal connection to Gael and to LaHave Bakery, she has chosen to entrust us with telling its story.

As Gael's older sister, I am one of the few people who has known Gael throughout her entire lifetime. I have personal knowledge of the bakery from its first imaginings to the present day, and have been privy to Gael's struggles and successes. I have witnessed the steps taken over the years to save the building, transform spaces, source ingredients locally, improve the livelihoods of staff, and more. I have also known all the other interviewees personally for many years, which enhanced each interview with an atmosphere of genuine openness and trust.

I (Susan) lived in Lunenburg County during the bakery's first two decades. I had the good fortune to keep shop at the LaHave Craft Co-op for several days during the summers of 1996 and 1997. The South Shore Waldorf School was a member at the time, and my children attended the school. I vividly recall loving every minute of it, exploring the displays of the various craftspeople and artists, meeting and serving customers, enjoying the view of the river through the large windows, and simply basking in the feel of the place. And it hasn't lost its magic for me. In more recent years, as Jane's wife, I've become more intimately connected with Gael, Sadie, Jesse, and the bakery.

Authoring this book together has been both an intense project and a rewarding one. In our naïveté, we didn't fully comprehend the magnitude and the responsibility of what we were taking on. We stayed the course, however, settling into a collaborative, harmonious process. We combined our shared love of words, writing, and reading with our individual perspectives and skills, to bring balance to the work and stay true to each "voice."

Documenting this oral history of LaHave Bakery has been a privilege. There are, essentially, two main characters in the story: proprietor Gael Watson, and the LaHave Outfitting Company building. Gael has selflessly invested decades of incredibly hard work, dedication, and commitment to the bakery, to the building that houses it, to customers, to her staff, and to her community. The building, built partially over the LaHave River, has a way of drawing people in, an energy that inspires many who cross its threshold. The exquisite craftsmanship in the shop is evocative of a bygone age, with its tin ceiling, stained-glass transom window, oak-panelled walls and shelves, plate glass cabinets, and old brass cash registers that are still in daily use. And then there's the bakery, with the tastes and smells of delicious fresh bread, delectable sweets, lunches made to order, and freshly made coffee. The colourful menu boards entice, the stairs leading to other areas, up and down, beckon. More surprises and feasts await the eyes, the appetite, the mind, and the spirit, beyond the front door.

LaHave Bakery is Gael Watson's living legacy. For nearly four decades, people from all walks of life have travelled from near and far, by land and by sea, to the community of LaHave, Lunenburg County, Nova Scotia, to experience the bakery for themselves. At long last, the story of the iconic LaHave Bakery has been committed to print.

Welcome to *LaHave Bakery: The Building, the Baker, and the Recipes that Revitalized a Community.* Come on in and enjoy!

Jane Morrigan and Susan Ivany,
March 2024

Voices

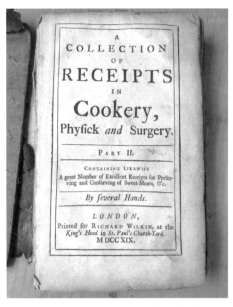

AN ANCIENT COOKBOOK, PRINTED IN 1719 and treasured by Gael Watson, proprietor of LaHave Bakery, states that it was written "by several hands." Similarly, *LaHave Bakery: The Building, the Baker, and the Recipes that Revitalized a Community* is told "by several voices."

Meet the cast of characters whose individual voices are interwoven to tell this colourful story.

A page from the 1719 cookbook that is treasured by Gael Watson.

GLORIA BARRETT Resident of LaHave, Lunenburg County, NS, since the 1970s; graduate of the Nova Scotia College of Art and Design (NSCAD) in Halifax, NS; well-known painter; former twenty-one-year employee of LaHave Bakery; maintained a close personal friendship with Gael Watson. Gloria Barrett passed away in Bridgewater, NS, on October 5, 2023.

KATHRYN GORDON Resident of nearby West Dublin, Lunenburg County, NS; accomplished glass artisan; former partner in the purchase of the LaHave Outfitting Company, Ltd. building; member of the LaHave Craft Co-operative since its inception in 1993; former bookkeeper and sweets baker for the bakery; friend of Gael Watson.

PEGGY GREER
Resident of West Dublin, Lunenburg County, NS; able sailor; spent many years involved with Covey Island Boatworks; former employee of LaHave Bakery; one of Gael Watson's first supporters and a good friend.

SADIE WATSON
Resident of West LaHave, Lunenburg County, NS; graduate of Dalhousie University, Halifax, NS; population health promoter with the Nova Scotia Health Authority; community development activist; part-time administration support for LaHave Bakery; Gael Watson's daughter.

BEV KAULBACK
Resident of Crousetown, Lunenburg County, NS; baker at LaHave Bakery; neighbour and friend of Gael Watson.

JESSE WATSON
Resident of West Dublin, NS; artist; owner–operator of Homegrown Skateboards; community activist and advocate; Gael Watson's son.

LAURA PITTS
Resident of Broad Cove, Lunenburg County, NS; graduate of Memorial University of Newfoundland, St. John's, NL; manager of LaHave Bakery; editor of Compliments Digest, the weekly staff newsletter.

GAEL WATSON
Resident of Crousetown, Lunenburg County, NS; owner/operator of LaHave Bakery; avid gardener.

ANDRA WHITE
Resident of Dublin Shore, Lunenburg County, NS; bookkeeper for LaHave Bakery; co-owner of LaHave River Books; friend of Gael Watson.

PART 1

Before the Bakery

CHAPTER 1

History of the LaHave Outfitting Company Building, 1901–1984

IT IS VERY IMPORTANT TO GAEL THAT THE HISTORY OF THE LAHAVE OUTFITTING Company building, locally known as "LaHave Outfitters," be told. She has learned much about it since beginning the LaHave Bakery nearly forty years ago. Gael has been inspired by the old stories she's been told and by the old records she's found—stories about the "salt for salt fish" trade, outfitting, and about Fraser Gray. The ledgers, invoices, receipts, letters, telegrams, photos, and reports retrieved from nooks and crannies in the building reveal a way of life and a way of doing business in the early twentieth century in LaHave. This chapter offers documented support that will provide context for topics that come up throughout the book.

PROPERTY OWNERS SINCE 1900

1900 – George Conrad sold the property to Laughlin B. Currie, merchant, for five hundred dollars.

1901 – The present-day building was constructed by Boehner Bros. Woodworking of West LaHave, for Laughlin B. Currie, merchant.

Fraser Gray. (FISHERIES MUSEUM OF THE ATLANTIC, LUNENBURG, NS, F87.142.1)

1903 – Laughlin B. Currie leased the building to Gilbert S. Troop for Black Bros. & Co.; the lease was for five years, at a rate of seven hundred dollars per year.

1911 – L. B. Currie Estate sold to Alfred Jones and A. H. Whitman, Halifax merchants.

1912 – Alfred Jones and A. H. Whitman sold to the LaHave Outfitting Company, Ltd.

1917 – LaHave Outfitting Company, Ltd. sold to Fraser Gray, merchant.

1953 – Fraser Gray sold to Teleen and Lawrence Gray.

1984 – Teleen and Lawrence Gray sold to Russ and Kathryn Gordon and Michael and Gael Watson.

1985 – Russ and Kathryn Gordon sold their share to Michael and Gael Watson.

2002 – Michael Watson sold his share to Gael Watson.

2002 – Gael Watson became the sole proprietor of LaHave Bakery.

SALT FISH TRADE

The "bank" fishery was a driving force of the Lunenburg County economy from the late 1800s into the early 1900s. It involved long fishing trips by schooners to the Grand Banks, one of the richest fishing grounds in the world. The fish, mainly cod, was caught from dories, and after having heads, guts, and backbones removed, was heavily salted, layer by layer, in the vessel's hold at sea. Upon return to shore, the salted fish was cured by drying at a fish plant, or "fish-maker," as they were called. It was first washed, then piled to allow the brine to drain, and then spread on racks called "flakes" to dry in the sun.[1]

Fishing was done by one of two methods: dory trawling or handlining. In dory trawling, each double dory crew set a baited, one mile–long trawl line that was anchored and marked by buoys at both ends. One fisher "underran" the trawl by removing the fish from the hooks, and the other re-baited the line. The whole procedure would be repeated several times a day, depending on the weather. Once the dory was full, it would be rowed back to the schooner and unloaded. Alternatively, handlining was reportedly the common method of fishing at the Port of LaHave. By this method, a fisher worked alone in a small dory, handling two or three lines, raising them up and down on either side of the dory, catching fish. This method used less bait, and as James S. Richard of Getson Cove observed in 1877, "Trawling I consider very bad for the fishery, as the mother fish are taken and great quantities of spawn are destroyed."[2]

In 1899, there were 166 Lunenburg County vessels engaged in the bank fishery. Each typically carried a twenty-one–person crew consisting of the captain, mate, cook, salter, throater, header, "flunkie," and fourteen fishers divided into seven double dory crews.[3] (The throater's job was to cut the throat of each fish to bleed it out, then split the fish halfway; the header then removed the head and guts and saved the liver for the oil; the fish was then split and the backbone removed; finally, the salter covered each layer of fish with salt; the flunkie was a person who did odd jobs.)

Growth in the bank fishery, as compared to inshore, was due to a trend toward building larger vessels that could hold more fish. Schooners were suited to the rough seas of the Atlantic Ocean, and typically made two trips—one lasting two months to the Western Banks in spring, and a longer trip of three months to the Newfoundland Grand Banks in fall. This practice of staying at sea for months at a time was due, in part, to federal incentives called "fishing bounties," which were designed to help the industry better compete with foreign fishing vessels. For example, every fisher working on a fishing vessel for a minimum of three months received a three-dollar "bounty" once a year.[4]

The strength of the Lunenburg County fishing fleet was that it was self-contained, meaning that vessels were locally built, owned, outfitted, and crewed. There were numerous opportunities for local seafarers, labourers, sailmakers, blacksmiths, farmers, coopers, shipbuilders, and others to participate.[5]

The Port of LaHave was a busy hub during the early 1900s. For example, in 1909 the fishing fleet of LaHave landed 45,000 quintals (a quintal is a 112-pound or 50-kg unit) of fish, selling at $4.00 to $4.50 per quintal.[6] The LaHave River

LaHAVE, N. S., Sept. 6, 1918.

ACCOUNT NO.
LETTER | FOLIO

M_____ SCHR. "MARGARET MOULTON."

FISH COMPANY ACCOUNT #2.

BOUGHT OF **LaHave Outfitting Co., Ltd.**

General Merchants

Terms, Interest charged on Overdue Accounts

HARDWARE AND FISHING SUPPLIES

DATE	ARTICLES #1.	FOLIO	CREDIT AMOUNT	DEBIT AMOUNT	TOTAL
Sept.6	3/4 doz. Knives & Forks 1.60 3/4 doz. Tra Spoons .70			2 30	
	1 " Table Spoons .60 2 Large Chimneys 6.30			1 20	
	2 Medium Chimneys @.28 2 Tin Pans @.10			76	
	2 Enam. Pans @.80 2 Sugar Bowls @.40 1 Butter Dish .20			2 60	
	1 Enam. Bowl .90 4 Tin Pans 3/.20, 1/.25			1 75	
	1 Tin Pint .40 1 Earthen Bean Crock .40			80	
	1 " Lamp .60 2 Enam. Bowls @.30			1 20	
	2 Tin Covers 1/.07, 1/.10 2 Tea Pots @1.35			2 87	
	3 Enam. Pots 1/1.50, 1/1.70, 1/1.40 2 Dust Pans @.20			5 00	
	1 Sheat Iron Bread Pan .90 2 Fire Shovels @.35			1 60	
	1 Flour Sieve .20 1 Cuspidor .45 1 Enam. Pitcher 1.30			1 95	
	2 Funnels 1/.40, 1/.15 1 Wash Basin .50			1 05	
	1 Fry Pan .50 1 Enam. Water Kettle 2.25			2 75	
	1 Skimmer .40 2 Large Tops @.25 1 Soup Ladle .45			1 35	
	6 Lamp Wicks .05 1 Egg Beater .20 1 M. Spoon .20			45	
	1 Potato Masher .25 1 Lantern 1.25 9 Mugs @.25			3 75	
	2 Earthen Bowls @.25 9 - 9 in. Plates @2.00			2 00	
	9 - 8 in. Plates @1.90 9 - 7 " " @1.80			2 78	
	2 prs. 9 1/2 ft. Oars @1.70 1 - 18 in. Stillson Wrench 3.00			5 90	
	1 pr. 12 ft. Oars 2.50 2 Trawl Lines @1.90			6 30	
	6 Soup Plates 2.00 4 yds. Towelling @.20			1 80	50 16

A LaHave Outfitting Company record of provisions for the schooner Margaret Moulton, *1918, found and archived by Gael Watson.* ৵

often had fifty to sixty schooners anchored during the heyday of the salt fishery. A record of the "Hailings of the LaHave Fishing Fleet" for the 1917 season shows a total of 121,305 quintals of fish (13,586,160 pounds) from forty-six schooners.[7]

The "West Indies" trade consisted of exporting salt cod to the Caribbean region and purchasing fishery salt, molasses, rum, and other goods for the return journey from various trading partners along the route.[8] Caribbean salt ponds, called salinas, supplied the New England, Nova Scotia, and Newfoundland fishing economies with salt,[9] which was typically transported as ballast on board a ship. Gael Watson was once told that freighting loose salt was a "strain on the staunchest sailing vessels," because the cargo was loaded "up to the hatch covers," and any leakage tended to clog the ship's pumps with a "viscous solution of brine."

The salt fish trade depended on securing a large amount of salt to preserve the fish that was caught. Two pounds of salt was required to dry one pound of cod.[10] In Nova Scotia, very little salt was produced locally prior to the twentieth century. It wasn't until 1912 that salt brine was discovered in a well in Malagash, Cumberland County.[11] In the days of the enormous cod fishery, Lunenburg County fishing companies typically purchased salt from the Turks and Caicos Islands in the Caribbean.[12] Tons and tons of salt were bought and stored in the LaHave Outfitting Company building, which was built using extra ships' knees (the root and trunk of a spruce tree that form a very strong right angle) for support. These ships' knees can still be seen in the bookstore—LaHave River Books—and in the LaHave Craft Co-op area.

Fishery salt continued to be purchased by the LaHave Outfitting Company until at least 1923. There is a record for that year, found in the building by Gael Watson, of 6,725 bushels that were picked up from Frith Bros. & Company of Grand Turk, Turks Island, West Indies, for the price of 10¢ per bushel, totaling $672.50.

OUTFITTERS

At the turn of the twentieth century, numerous "outfitters," also known as "ship chandlers," supplied provisions and other services needed by vessels and crews involved in the fishery. The origin of the word chandler goes back further in time, meaning "candle seller." Outfitters were often also general merchants, serving the local community. LaHave Outfitting Company was one of several outfitters situated along the LaHave River in the early part of the century.

A sampling of provisions available at the LaHave Branch of Atlantic Fish Companies, Ltd., taken from a 1909 detailed inventory of stock, included items such as pickaxes, yellow sugar, fence wire, Stanfield's underwear, brooms, lamp chimneys, ship scrapers, chain, duck cloth, paint, sheep shears, cow bells, butter, eggs, oar locks, and shoe nails. Also available were caulking mallets, dory compasses, rivets, buckles, harpoons, trawl swivels, rope, yarn, fishing lines, roll roofing, Quaker Oats, Swift's Soap, olive oil, oil clothing, molasses, vinegar, shovels, canned milk, coal tar, pork shoulders, kippered herring, macaroni, mustard, hops, Finnan Haddie, cornstarch, yeast cakes, chocolate, milk pails, Magic Baking Powder, tea, bean crocks, raisins, pickles, beans, and biscuits.

SHARING PROFITS AND LOSSES

As a way of limiting personal loss if a vessel was lost at sea or had a poor fishing season, it was customary during the early twentieth century for a vessel to be co-owned by the managing owner, local investors, and sometimes crew members, so profits and losses could be shared.[13]

Also, revenue from fishing trips to the Grand Banks was often shared on a co-operative basis between a vessel's owners and crew. All of the crew worked on shares, with the exception of the header, throater, and cook. The salter and the captain were each entitled to a share in addition to a commission. The revenue could be shared one of three ways: equally—the simplest and preferred way when the crew were known to be good workers; by count, based on the number of fish in each dory crew's catch; or by weight of the fish in each dory crew's catch, which was the favoured way when the quality of the workers was unknown. First, however, the captain's commission, the header's and throater's wages, the cost of bait and ice, the cost of fish-making at the plants, and the cost of delivery were deducted from the gross earnings of the catch. The owners were responsible for paying the major costs of outfitting, including provisions, salt, and fishing gear. After these charges were met, the owners' portion was divided and issued as dividends on the shares. Crew members paid the cook's wages, marine insurance, and other costs incidental to the voyage out of their share of the revenue.[14]

The amount of money each fisher cleared varied, depending on personal expenses. Those expenses could include their personal supplies while at sea—things such as a medicine chest, tobacco, candy, and liquor, as well as items purchased and put on their tab at the company store. An example from the records of 1906 found in the building shows a payment to Russel Hirtle, who fished aboard the schooner *Atlantic*, of $69.28. Once personal expenses were subtracted, he received $12.76. For the same trip, Allison Corkum was paid $55.32. After his personal expenses were deducted, he received $45.32.

THE EARLY YEARS IN THE BUILDING, 1901–1912

On March 5, 1901, Laughlin B. Currie of West Dublin announced plans to build warehouses and wharves in LaHave to conduct a West Indies trade, and to also operate as a general merchant.[15] The building was constructed that same year, by Boehner Bros. Woodworking of West LaHave. Fraser Gray, who would become the owner of the building one day, began employment as a clerk for L. B. Currie, and was there for the opening of the store on September 15, 1901.[16]

Outfitting of fishing vessels, large and small, was a large part of the business in the early years. In an article written by Fraser Gray, published in the September 22, 1954, edition of the *Bridgewater Bulletin*, he recalled that "the exporting of fish and other products was carried on for several years, and local trade with fishermen and the public was extensive."

Laughlin Currie retired in 1903. He leased the building for five years to Black Bros. & Co. of Halifax, who continued the outfitting and general merchant business there. Black Bros. & Co. also had a large fish factory at Getsons Cove, less than a mile away. Their manager, Gilbert S. Troop, was likely in charge of both locations.

In 1904, Laughlin Currie died. One year later, Black Bros. & Co. was foreclosed on.[17] Two years later, Black Bros. & Co. amalgamated with other fish export companies to form Atlantic Fish Companies, Ltd., headquartered in Lunenburg, NS,[18] with the "LaHave Branch" apparently operating out of both the L. B. Currie building and the former Black Bros. & Co. fish plant. When the five-year lease expired in 1908, Fraser Gray took over as managing director of the LaHave Branch of Atlantic Fish Companies, Ltd.

In 1911, L. B. Currie's estate sold the building to Halifax merchants Jones and Whitman, who were associated with Atlantic Fish Companies, Ltd. The following year, the building was sold again, this time to the newly formed LaHave Outfitting Company, of which Fraser Gray was managing director.

LAHAVE OUTFITTING COMPANY, LTD., 1912–1984

For sixty-three years, Fraser Gray was the one constant in the life of the LaHave Outfitters building, from the day the doors opened in 1901 until his death in 1964. He was born on January 30, 1874, in West Dublin, Lunenburg County, NS. At age thirteen, Fraser began his career as a fisher. His first voyage was a three-month fishing trip to the Grand Banks on the schooner *Rialto*. He was paid eight dollars a month plus food and lodging. Eleven years later, in 1898, while on passage from the West Indies to Boston aboard the schooner *L. B. Currie*, he survived a severe storm that went down in history as the Portland Gale.[19] It was named after the SS *Portland*, a steamship that sank in that storm,

The LaHave Outfitting Company expansion, which included a smokehouse at end of the wharf, c. 1935. (UNKNOWN)

taking with it all passengers and crew—an estimated 193 people. Many ships and boats, along with their crews and passengers, were lost that day all along the Eastern Seaboard.[20] And so, by the age of twenty-four, Fraser Gray decided that making a living at sea was not for him. His fishing days soon came to an end. In 1901, he began his involvement with the building that, today, still bears the name LaHave Outfitting Company, Ltd.

Fraser Gray was instrumental in the formation of the LaHave Outfitting Company, Ltd., which was registered with the Nova Scotia Registry of Joint Stock Companies in 1912. He was well positioned to lead the new enterprise when the Atlantic Fish Companies business went into decline in LaHave and their operations at the fish plant at Getsons Cove ceased.

The LaHave Outfitting Company carried out a large fish export business and operated as an outfitter, fish plant, general merchant, and grocer. The company supplied up to twenty-five schooners a season, and owned shares in a number of them.[21] Its letterhead stated, "General Outfitters and Dealers in Fishing Supplies. Satisfaction Guaranteed." In the same September 1954 *Bridgewater Bulletin* newspaper article, Fraser Gray stated that "between 1912 and 1930, LaHave Outfitting Company did a very large business furnishing foodstuffs and fishing supplies to the many Bank fishing schooners and freighters that were in operation at the time."

The LaHave Outfitting Company used telegrams to arrange to hire fishing captains, crews, and cooks for its fleet of schooners, and for other vessel owners as well. In 1928, for example, telegrams were sent between the company and Captain Thomas Pardy of Harbour Breton, NL. The company wished to "engage eight dory crews, experienced trawl fishermen." Captain Pardy was assured that the vessel was "one of best, two years old." Several such telegrams found in the building by Gael Watson illustrate the regular business practices between sea merchants and fishing captains and crews in the early decades of the twentieth century.

In 1915, Fraser Gray became a shareholder, along with J. E. Bachman and David Bachman of Riverport, of an additional company, LaHave Fish Company, Ltd. This company carried on the outfitting business at the LaHave Outfitters building, as well as at the former Black Bros. & Co. fish plant at Getsons Cove. In 1923, that company came to an end when, on August 20, all six buildings of the LaHave Fish Company factory at Getsons Cove burned to the ground. It was reported that a lot of fishing gear, some dories, cable, and a quantity of salt were in the buildings at the time. Also, the large pier was partially demolished. No trace of the cause of the fire was discovered.[22]

In 1917, a sign appeared on the front stoop of the LaHave Outfitting Company building, stating, "The Canadian Bank of Commerce Will Open a Branch Upstairs Shortly." The bank operated there until about 1922, when it moved across the road to a new brick building. Also in 1917, Fraser Gray became owner of the LaHave Outfitting Company and property, and remained a key figure in the running of the business at the building for nearly the next fifty years.

LaHave Outfitting Company records from 1925 show that employees were paid 25¢ an hour. A sampling of employees' names included Johnson Wilkie, Wilson Himmelman, Freeman Publicover, Elias Corkum, and Charles Feener. Also, assets listed for that year show that the building and wharf were valued at $7,420. Company records from 1933 show the labour cost to pack fish was 27¢ an hour. In 1934, small cod were purchased for 1¢ per pound from local fishers. Some of the surnames were Wolfe, Rhodenhizer, Pentz, Corkum, Richard, Maschke, Hubley, Wilkie, Romkey, and Hirtle.

With the decline of the salt fishery, the LaHave Outfitting Company, along with many other sea merchants, suffered some severe financial losses. In a 1958 newspaper interview, Fraser Gray recalled that there were "bargain sales on dozens of ships."

Fraser Gray, proprietor, and Freeman Richard at the front door of the LaHave Outfitting Company, c. 1952. (UNKNOWN)

"In 1930, we sold a 175-ton schooner to the West Indies for $2,000, just to pay debts. Five and six years before they had cost as much as $30,000."[23]

In the midst of the Depression, the LaHave Outfitting Company was struggling with a decline in business. According to Fraser Gray, the "Bank fishing fleet of schooners that operated from LaHave and vicinity became extinct in 1935."[24] The annual report of 1936 stated, "No vessels operating from this Port means none to outfit," a trend seen over the previous few years. The report also stated that the dry and pickled fish business "proved very unprofitable."

In 1934, Fraser Gray had considered selling the business. In the end, he opted to try to turn the business around. Refrigeration had altered the fishing industry dramatically, and the LaHave Outfitting Company decided a more modern operation was the answer to remaining in business. In 1935, the company borrowed $10,000 to purchase and install a freezing and cold-storage plant in the building.

The upgrade to the business consisted of four freezer rooms, an engine room, a smokehouse, a shed, and an ice house. Each independently controlled freezer room contained numerous continuous tubular coils. Ammonia was pumped through the coils of one room to "sharp-freeze" the fresh fish at -25°F, and through the remaining three rooms to store the frozen fish products. The engine room contained the ammonia compressor, condenser, receiver, and pumping engine. Although electricity was available at the time, Fraser Gray found that the Nova Scotia Power Commission's rate was "exorbitant." So, instead of installing an electric motor, he opted for a Fairbanks Morse diesel engine fueled by crude oil.[25] It was reputed to be a very loud machine.

Their business now consisted of purchasing fresh fish from local fishers, preparing and freezing it, and selling it to local and more distant markets. It was marketed and distributed under the label, "LaHave Fish, of LaHave Outfitting Co.," with the logo, "LaHave on the Label Means Good Fish on the Table."

The company continued to operate the fish plant until about 1949. By then, the decline in the fishing and shipping industries led to the downsizing of the whole operation. LaHave Outfitters continued mainly as a general merchant and grocery store in the village of LaHave into the 1960s. The deed to the building and control of the company were transferred from Fraser Gray to his sons, Teleen and Lawrence, in 1953.

Fraser Gray remained active in the business until a year or two before his death in 1964. From then on, Teleen and Lawrence Gray kept the business going until they sold the building to four young "come-from-away" entrepreneurs in December 1984.

THE *JUTLAND*

The *Jutland* was a fishing vessel that met a tragic end on the Western Grand Banks on March 11, 1920. It was a wooden 136-ton beam trawler, powered by a steam engine, built in 1918–19 by Boehner Bros. of West LaHave. The vessel was co-owned by four sea merchants from the LaHave area: J. E. Bachman, Fraser Gray, M. J. Parks, and J. N. Rafuse & Sons.

When the *Jutland* left Liverpool, NS, on or near February 25, there were twenty-one men on board. Captain Johnson, along with mate John Ellison and nineteen crew members, were mostly from Liverpool and the surrounding South Shore communities. According to a *Halifax Chronicle Herald* newspaper article dated March 12, 1920, heavy seas prevented the crew of the *Jutland* from catching any fish and disabled the steering gear. The *Jutland* put in to Halifax for the repair, and during the four days in port, some of the crew left. Captain Johnson sent to Liverpool for more men to replace them, and the ship cleared Customs House in Halifax on March 2 with twenty-one men on board.

CASUALTY.

Where casualty happened.							Result of casualty.			
Exact spot.	Name of country or sea.	Date and hour.	State of tide	State of weather and atmosphere.	Direction and force of wind.	State of sea and in what direction flowing	Total loss. State value, if known.	Partial loss. State estimated loss.	No. of lives lost.	No. of lives saved and by what means.
23.	24.	25.	26.	27.	28.	29	30.	31.	32.	33
not Known	north Atlantic	—	—	—	—	—	Total Loss. Value, $ 210 000 ⁰⁰	—	all hands lost	

If salvage services were rendered, state by whom.	Brief account of casualty with remarks as to cause, and whether it could have been avoided, also nature and extent of damage to ship and cargo.
34.	35.
	Beam Trawler SS Jutland - sailed from Halifax NS March 2ⁿᵈ 1920 on a fishing voyage for. Western Banks. She was last seen on Western Bank on March 10ᵗ. On March 11ᵗ one of the Jutland dories was picked up containing the dead body of the mate. Nothing further has been heard respecting this vessel.

A portion of the casualty report for the sinking of the Jutland, March 1920. *Twenty-one crew members were lost.* (JANE MORRIGAN) ᴄ⅋ᴼ

On Wednesday, March 10, the *Jutland* was seen on the fishing grounds by an American trawler. On Thursday evening, March 11, one hundred miles to the southeast of Halifax, a Halifax trawler named *Lemberg* came across two dories, some distance apart, belonging to the *Jutland*. One of the dories was swamped and broken, with its painter cut, and contained the dead body of a man, later identified by a crew member of the *Lemberg* as the *Jutland*'s mate, John Ellison. Apart from the two damaged dories and the body of John Ellison, who died of exposure according to a Halifax medical examiner, there were no survivors, and no other trace of the *Jutland* was ever found. As stated in the same article, "There is now little doubt in the minds of marine men here but that the *Jutland*'s name can be placed on the list of good ships cut down by the terrible gales which swept the North Atlantic within the past two weeks."

RUM-RUNNING IN NOVA SCOTIA

Smuggling rum from the Caribbean was a long-standing, profitable tradition in Nova Scotia, closely tied to the commercial relationships borne of the "salt for

THE *JUTLAND*: A CURIOUS CATCH

On the fishing trip just prior to the fateful sinking of the *Jutland*, the crew had trawled an uncommon anchor from the bottom of the sea. In fact, it was a pair of anchors, crossed and fused together. It was brought back to shore. A veteran of the Royal Navy, Captain Patch, a prominent citizen of Liverpool, initiated a funding drive to build a memorial to the sailors whose lives were lost on the *Jutland*. He approached the owners of the vessel, one of whom was Fraser Gray, asking to have the mysterious crossed anchors used as part of the memorial. The owners gladly donated them.

The monument was created and installed at the Old Burying Grounds on Main Street in Liverpool in 1920. An inscription was engraved on a marble plaque and fastened to a large rock. It reads: "God's Mercy—Our Hope" and "In memory of the crew of the Beam Trawler *Jutland*. Foundered at Sea March 11, 1920. These crossed anchors recovered from fishing banks on *Jutland*'s previous trip are placed as a symbol of our hope that their souls are resting in eternal peace."[26]

salt fish" trade. The era of Prohibition began when the Temperance movement pushed for laws that would abolish "evil alcohol." In 1910, the Nova Scotia Legislature passed the Temperance Act. The law applied to all areas of Nova Scotia except Halifax, which was eventually included six years later. In the United States in January 1920, a ban was placed on the manufacture, sale, and transportation of all intoxicating beverages. This development created a new and more lucrative opportunity for Nova Scotia fishers, boat owners, and others to sell smuggled liquor to American buyers waiting on "Rum Row," just outside the three-mile limit in international waters.[27]

Prohibition impacted the Nova Scotia fishery significantly. It became very difficult to find crew for fishing voyages to the Grand Banks. Newfoundland captains and crews were sought after by sea merchants such as LaHave Outfitting Company to take the place of the many local South Shore fishers who became involved in rum-running. In a May 13, 2002, *Maclean's* article by John DeMont, ninety-year-old Clement Hiltz of Lunenburg recalled, "I could make more money running one load of booze than I could in a year on the fishing boats."

Rum was acquired mostly from the West Indies, and hard liquor—Canadian whisky in particular—was often purchased from the French islands of Saint-Pierre and Miquelon, off the south coast of Newfoundland. Rum-running was an illicit yet very profitable business for those who were willing to risk being caught, or even killed, by the authorities who came after them in high-powered boats. In one infamous incident near Lunenburg in 1933, the 40-foot rum-runner boat *Silver Arrow* was approached by a coast guard cutter in which agent Machine Gun Kelly shot and killed Billie Tanner. By 1930, the conflicts between rum-runners, the police raids, and the involvement of organized crime, including the notorious Al Capone, had proven that Prohibition was unpopular. Ultimately, it was viewed by the majority of the Nova Scotia public as too dangerous to be continued. Prohibition in Nova Scotia formally came to an end in 1930 with the passage of the Liquor Control Act.[28] Rum-running and bootlegging, however, continued long after.

PART 2

LaHave Bakery: The Early Years

CHAPTER 2

Beginnings

LAHAVE IN 1984

Gloria Barrett

WHAT WAS LAHAVE LIKE? LAHAVE WAS A SECRET, THE BEST-KEPT SECRET. Wonderful. There was nothing, which is why I came. It was great. There was no garbage collection in LaHave, there was no active fire hall gang, and there was no doctor. The LaHave Outfitters building was a skeleton. It was empty, and it wasn't heated. One of the Gray brothers would go in everyday with his necktie and his V-neck cardigan and man the place. And you could go in and ask for something. A can of dog food that had been there since 1942. There was nothing fresh, let's say. As soon as LaHave started to change, it happened very rapidly. And the bakery, the beginning of the bakery, made a lot of things happen. Good things. I couldn't believe that we were going to have a bakery. I couldn't believe that this place was going to not die. I wanted solitude, but I didn't want to be in the graveyard.

Gael Watson

Down the road, Creaser's clothing factory, where they made rain gear, sou'westers, and working gear, had closed down. Himmelman Supply Company next door was no longer operating. At the Outfitters, Teleen Gray [son of former

Gael Watson, Sadie Watson, and Mike Watson in front of the LaHave Outfitting Company building just after purchasing it in December 1984. (LEIGH ROBERTSON)

owner Fraser Gray] was there every day, but there was not a lot of active business. There was the ferry, of course, going back and forth across the LaHave River. The post office was there and the Royal Bank, and that was about it. And Gloria's studio—Gloria Barrett. She'd been there for many years, painting every day, selling her paintings in the summer. There were still a lot of elderly people living in LaHave. There were families who lived year-round along the route. However, there were also a lot of people from places like Ontario, Germany, the States, who were buying houses but weren't living in them full-time. So it was pretty quiet, LaHave.

AN AMAZING BUILDING

Gael Watson

I might as well go back to the very beginning. How the building came into our lives. In the summer and fall of 1983, Mike's former boss, Lawrence Himmelman, said he was going to be tearing down the warehouse on their property next door to the LaHave Outfitters. Mike said, "I'll give you a dollar and I'll take it down." Lawrence said, "All right," so Mike proceeded in his very neat way to take apart this huge warehouse, piece by piece, and bring it over to our land to build a barn. It was during this time that the Royal Bank manager across the road was watching all of this and was very impressed with the neatness of the job. I was pregnant with Sadie, and I was getting bigger and bigger, and the old warehouse was getting smaller and smaller. It was during this time that a "For Sale" sign went up on the LaHave Outfitting Company building. Mike came home and he was breathless, and he said, "LaHave Outfitters is for sale!" We must have talked all through the night about that amazing building and what a person could do with it.

A year passed—or almost a year. The building was falling down. Teleen Gray would go over there every day. He was almost totally blind, and his wife, Gala, was very concerned for him. Meanwhile, the wharf was being washed away. They also worried they would be liable if a boat was struck by a piece of wharf. So there was pressure on them, and it was Gala who twisted Teleen's arm and said, "Just let them have it. Give them a price they can't refuse." And that's what happened.

Within a week of Sadie's first birthday, in November 1984, we agreed on the price, which had come down considerably to a very small amount of money. The problem was that, at that point, the building was in such bad shape we would need immediately to have more money—enough to put a roof on it. There lay the dilemma.

Kathryn Gordon

Mike was helping us build our house when the opportunity to buy the LaHave Outfitters building came up. Gael was baking and selling her bread from her home. Gael and Mike asked Russ and I if we'd like to partner with them in acquiring the building. We were all young and full of energy. We went to the Royal Bank across the road where the manager, Mr. Gaudet, decided to take a chance on the four of us. He changed many of our lives around here because he seemed to believe that the young entrepreneurs were worth lending money to, even though we really didn't have much in the way of assets. I have always felt indebted to him for this.

Gael Watson

When Mike and I went to see Jean Gaudet at the Royal Bank, he said, "Okay, all right, what have you got as a down payment?"

"Nothing."

"Well, where are you working?"

"We're not working."

Mike was out of a job and I wasn't working; I had just had a baby. "Oh," he said, "so all right, you have a house, you can use your house as collateral."

"No, we don't want to take a risk on our house."

He said, "Well, you have to come up with something."

And that was when we suggested our four-wheel drive Massey-Ferguson tractor. He said, "I'll take it." So that's how we got it. The four of us bought the building from brothers Lawrence and Teleen Gray in December 1984.

Teleen Gray in the LaHave Outfitting Company shop, c. 1973. (UNKNOWN)

IN ROUGH SHAPE

Jesse Watson

I was seven years old when they bought the building. Being an outdoor kid, it was really inspiring and felt kind of like a gold mine for fort-building and making things. Getting into my earliest memories, there was another old building on the property that had fallen down. It was just a tangle of broken glass and boards and Styrofoam. I remember rummaging in there and pulling things out.

I started making forts on rafts and dragging them down on the beach. I'd get on the raft and get out on the water. I had a pole and I'd pole up and down along the beach, working with the tide. Lawrence and Ruby Gray, who lived next door, had a little wharf and I'd tie up to that and visit with them. A very distinct memory is the bottom floor, where the old fish-drying rooms were. You just walked along and the floorboards slowly slanted down and became an intersection of lapping waves and floorboards. That's the only way to describe it—it was like an internal beach. It smelled of the outdoors; it smelled like the riverbanks; it smelled like mussel shells; it smelled like seagulls and saltiness. Not quite a cave, not a beach, not a building—all these places in one. And I was just watching the water pull out on these planks, and I was like, "Wow, that's going to take some fixing." And each floor did that, but that was the bottom floor, so it met the tide. These floors just went out and were just cut off, pulled off. I still have dreams about what the second floor felt like as well. Just corridors of stuff, combinations of salvage things, shipping things. Not on the radar yet for Mike and Gael to deal with; they were too busy up front with the space that would be the shop and the bakery.

Gael Watson

Early memories of it, the smell of it, the smell of gear—fishing gear and rope. It was a pervasive industrial smell of what had been going on there all those years before. There are times when I can still smell it, faintly. Not that I didn't like the smell, but it wasn't really fitting with a food store. It's hard to describe, but I remember thinking, "How am I ever going to change the smell?" But, amazingly enough, within a week of baking the bread, the bread took over; the smell of bread took over.

Gloria Barrett

It was an old building that had freezers in it, drying fish, and boats coming and going. When they bought it, it was nothing, it was just falling down. It was just a breath from being what you collect at the curb when the garbage truck goes by.

The condition of the shop in 1984—beautiful cabinetry, original hardwood floor, tin ceiling. (UNKNOWN)

Kathryn Gordon

The front section of the building needed almost no work. It was like a beautiful museum, with everything perfectly preserved. Beautiful stained glass, pressed tin ceiling, lovely rich woodwork, beautiful old counters. The safes. The back of the building, however, from behind the storefront to the wharf, was in hard shape.

Gael Watson

The shop was a beautiful illustration of the kind of workmanship that people put into shopfronts at the end of the 1800s and the early 1900s, with a lot of close-fitting, narrow, tongue-and-groove, shellacked walls and wide wooden counters. The hardwood floor in the shop has been there since the building was built in 1901. We're talking over a hundred and twenty years that the shop has been used pretty much without stopping. It may have slowed down a bit

The LaHave Outfitting Company building facing the LaHave River, December 1984. Jesse Watson and Gael Watson stand near the door; Sadie Watson is in the baby carrier. (LEIGH ROBERTSON)

from time to time, but it never came to a full stop. Those floors have had people walking over them with sandy or salty or dirty boots and shoes—even bare feet—and they are still absolutely straight and strong.

I remember that first winter because it was harsh. The whitecaps were on the river. I got to know LaHave in a way that I had never noticed before. It was the mighty LaHave River, especially at that point with the tide coming in and the weather coming in. It was a wild spot, and that building was moving with the weather. It was moving; it was groaning and creaking.

SAVING THE BUILDING

Gael Watson

We immediately started the saga of saving the building. By that time, part of the end of the building had collapsed into the river, and the wharf had washed out to sea. The 110-foot-long wall facing southeast was swinging in the wind. We had to tie it in with ropes. Most of the windows in the front were broken. It was in severe, rough shape.

Kathryn Gordon

As soon as we bought the building, we set to work fixing it up. The first thing we did was put a new roof on and, next, take apart the south wall of the building and replace it with new materials. It needed to be entirely reconstructed.

Gael Watson

Those initial repairs were made fairly quickly. The windows were replaced gradually, the shop was painted, and the end of the building was chainsawed off. The area below level, where the coal was kept, was dug out to make it deep enough to become the bread kitchen. It was amazing how quickly things happened; we got it in December and those things all happened by the early spring of 1985.

Kathryn Gordon

Gael decided that the best place for the bakery was the basement. I think probably because it would be cool, being underground. At the time, you could only just get into it; I don't think you could stand up. It had to be hand-dug, soil and rock taken out one wheelbarrow load at a time. Russ had a few of his carpenters to help with digging out the basement area.

What astounds me is so much work on the building happened in such a short time in order to get LaHave Bakery going. I was daunted by all of it, from the front store back. It seemed impossible.

One thing about Gael and Mike was that they both had great patience. They got a lot done. When we were all young, we were all getting a lot done, I found. They got a lot done in a short period of time, but they weren't ever in a panic.

Restoration of the south wall of the building. Russ Gordon standing on left, Mike Watson seated, and Lynne Carter standing on the right, c.1986. (PHIL CARTER)

GETTING DOWN TO BUSINESS

Gael Watson

In April, Mike was offered a job delivering a boat to Florida. We thought, "That's good. He's got a job, we need money, off you go." He was gone about two weeks when Russ came to me and said, "Kathryn and I have decided this is a much bigger investment than we're really prepared for. We would like to sell you our share." My feeling by that time was that it would be better for everybody. Partnerships are hard. We had different ideas. I agreed quite happily because they were good friends and I thought, "Sure, why not? Let's part on good terms."

By the first of May 1985, the building was now just Mike's and mine. Earlier, after the roof went on, we had had the building reappraised, and it was worth more, so we had borrowed more. Now, with two loans and the repayment to Russ and Kathryn for their share, it very quickly became quite a bit of money that Mike and I owed. Mike was away at sea for nine months. There was no money—no money at all coming in. But I had $5,000 in the bank account, and it was clear that now I was the only one who was going to do something. I had that $5,000.

❧

The bakery was my idea. We all had ideas about what we wanted to do, how we would do it, what our parts would be. Because I'd been baking down at the house, and because I'd even been selling some of the bread to neighbours, I thought if I was going to be involved, baking bread was a way I could contribute to that building. So that was my choice. "It's going to be the LaHave Bakery," I decided. That's the name because it's in LaHave.

Kathryn Gordon

Gael saw the entire bakery and storefront in her mind's eye right from the start. I remember walking through with her and Sadie when Sadie was only about one and a half years old, following Gael around in her striped coveralls. Gael would point out where her office was going to be, where the bread would be displayed, where to put the actual bakery.

Gael Watson

In May and June that year, I planted my garden as I usually did. I even stood up at one point after planting a row, and, looking at the neat rows, I said to the garden, "Don't worry, if I have to give anything up it'll be the bakery, not you." But, aux contraire, I had to give up the garden because I was fully, fully engaged with the bakery. I had no idea what I was getting into—totally oblivious to what it would take.

It really hit me with a clunk that I was responsible for making this thing work, and that I would lose so much if I couldn't. Personally, I felt like I would be to blame. It was all hanging on me, and if I couldn't make a go of it, that meant I was not capable. I was just full of lots of ideas; we could do this, I could do that. But I'd never run a business before.

So I walked into the office—the front office, where the accounting desk is—and I pulled out all the drawers and I stacked up the journals—all the accounting books that were there that ranged between 1915 and 1922. I turned the lamp on and started going through these ledgers, at first not even noticing what was in them. Then I started noticing. The moment that everything changed was when I was looking at not so much what was written in there, but what was in the margins, the pencil writings of long division and multiplication. They were just little, like when you're figuring something out in your head. Anyway, as soon as I saw the long division and the way that the person had done it, I thought, "I can do that. I can do that!" And then the multiplication, "I can do that. I understand that equation." And that led me to look at what was the "in" and the "out" and what the expenses were and what was at the bottom. I started turning the pages and I went through every ledger just looking at it, looking at it, taking it in until I closed the books, and put them back in the drawers. That was what taught me how to do business—those ledgers from that building, from that business— and I was going to be in the same building, and gradually the twenty-two or so people who worked in the fish plant, LaHave Outfitting Company and LaHave Fish Company, became twenty-two people working for the LaHave Bakery. It just went from fish to bread, but the same industriousness, the same energy, in the same building. It was pretty wonderful.

You learn. Everything I learn is always from somebody else. Those ledgers showed me that somebody knew how to do it; they made it from day to day, they made it from month to month, and the ledgers helped them to do that. That was truthful enough, that was solid enough for me to believe. If I could follow that, keep track of the "in" and the "out," that's all there is to it, really. You stay in business if you can pay your bills. That's the simplest business there is. You can do anything you want, for as long as you want, as long as you can pay your bills. And you're in!

Peggy Greer

I met Gael about two years before the bakery started, and I liked her very much. She was then, and still is, a brilliant and amazing person. When she told me she wanted to do this bakery, I thought it was a great idea. From the get-go, I thought it would work. I knew she could do it. When I heard that they were going to purchase the building, I admit I was envious. I had been wanting that amazing building. It has a soul that draws all people.

Gael Watson

It's the building that speaks. The energy is there, and it is what taught me, through its journals, how to do business. You know that expression, "If these walls could talk?" Those walls talk in a language that affects a lot of people. It's not just me being affected by this amazing building.

Gloria Barrett

I remember Gael came by. We sat on my front step together and she talked about what she was planning to do with the bakery. I'd never met her in my life. I didn't know who she was. She was homesteading nearby at that time. I liked her so much right away, so I wrote her a little note of intent. I told her that I believed in the bakery and said, "You'd be lucky if you hired me because I'm strong and ugly and I can do it." She got right back to me. Next thing I knew, I was hired.

Gael Watson

There were two old safes in the building. One was made by Goldie & McCulloch of Galt, Ontario, and it weighs probably a ton. The safe is very special. It's got eight-inch–thick doors that swing open, and inside the safe is another safe—a little one with beautiful mahogany drawers. It's just a beautiful piece of art.

I have a story about that safe. This was before the bakery opened. When we first got the building, we were given the combination, but I wanted to change it because I didn't know who all knew it. I had heard about a locksmith in Bridgewater, quite elderly. I called him up and said, "I've got this safe. Can you come and change the combination and show me how to use it?" He came that day. Later that night, I thought I'd better try to see if I can do this on my own. I kneeled down and dialed the combination, but I could not get it open. So I picked up the phone and called the man. It was quite late, about 10:00 P.M. I can't remember his name. I said, "I've tried in all different ways, but I can't get the safe open."

"Right," he said, "sit down beside the safe, put your ear to the door." He proceeded to tell me what to listen for and, following those instructions, it opened with a clunk. I said, "That's great, that's great; I've got it now. Thank you so much. Sorry to keep you up late tonight."

"Not a problem, not a problem," he said. The very next day, I learned that shortly after we talked, he had a massive heart attack and died! We were the only two who knew the combination to that safe. When he died, that left me as the only one who could open it.

◦◦◦

Also in the shop was the old cash register. It's a National cash register, patented in 1896, according to the bottom of the drawer. It's solid brass. It still works. We still use it. Those heavy brass ornate National cash registers were built right up until 1916. After that, all the metal went towards the war effort for the First World War. They never returned to building those heavy brass cash registers again.

◦◦◦

One day, while I was working in the garden, I saw a young man walking down the lane towards me. I thought he was a Jehovah's Witness, but it turned out he was the Hobart salesman who had heard that I was starting a bakery. He came to talk to me, and I said, "You don't even need to talk me into it. I've heard the Hobart mixer is the way to go, but the problem is the money. Can't afford it."

"Well, not a problem," he said. "You can pay for it by the month; you pay Hobart and there will be a service contract on it for the whole entire time that you're paying for it." And it cost more than $5,000, which you could buy a car for at that time, for this one piece of equipment. But it was the key, that Hobart mixer.

I was very impressed with him, the salesman who walked all the way down the lane, so I signed the contract for the Hobart. I had no idea how to use it. I had never made bread with a machine before, so I contacted Ed Levin of Ed Levin's Bakery in Mahone Bay, and he and his wife, Ruth, were happy to show me how to use the Hobart. That was great. But the Hobart I ordered wasn't arriving, and the day was getting closer and closer and closer, and "Where is the Hobart?" It finally arrived the day before I was to open, which meant I didn't have a chance to try it out first.

The kitchens were built and the bakery started. I tried for the opening day to be the first of July but it was actually a couple of weeks later. I remember at the time being really upset that, jeez, you know, we didn't make that deadline. But we still opened. We opened on July 26, 1985.

CHAPTER 3

Open for Business

OPENING DAY

Andra White

GAEL TALKS ABOUT HOW QUICKLY it went from spruce trees growing out of the roof to a building where she could open the doors.

Gael Watson

It was a gala day, beautiful, sunny. We had a piano in the shop, an upright, that my friend Eric Hustvedt played. I promised every customer a free strawberry custard tart. Rhonda McKearney was working with me on that first day. It was a crazy day, but very successful, wonderful. Lots and lots of support. It encouraged me; it made me think, "I can do this!"

Gael Watson in front of the LaHave Bakery shop. The bakery sign on the hook was hand-painted by her aunt, Rhoda Davidson, c. 1986. (UNKNOWN)

Kathryn Gordon

I have a few memories of the early days of the LaHave Bakery. The first one was opening day and Eric Hustvedt playing the piano as customers came in to buy bread and get their free strawberry tart. So many people came! The bakers were churning out tarts all day long!

Gael Watson

I have always smoked a fair amount of pot. My good friend, Marion Garlick, was quite a pot smoker, too, so we would get together and make plans for doing certain things, and it was always infused with this joie de vivre. One day we thought, "We need to come up with a guest list for the first day of the bakery." We had so much fun putting it together. It was hilarious. I still laugh when I remember it. Pierre Elliott Trudeau was on the list. A few of our favourite musicians, including Anne Murray, Edith Butler, and Bob Dylan. There were local people, too, like Jean Gaudet and Alexa McDonough. There was Janice Gill, from River John, the author of one of my favourite cookbooks, the *Canadian Bread Book*.

WHO'S GOING TO BUY THE BREAD?

Peggy Greer

In the beginning, there was a fair bit of doubt about the survival of a bakery in a tiny community. Who's going to buy the bread? The community did buy the bread, maybe even those who thought it would never work. Many of the locals, including the older people, began to come in and take pride in what was happening. They had been watching a community dying and had the great fortune of watching it resurrect.

The rhythm of the bakery has changed over the years. It's a bit like the sea. In the beginning, when it was seasonal, the tide of tourists rushed in during the summer and the local customers receded a bit. Then the wave of summer people left, and the locals came in again to keep it all going a little longer each year. Thanks to Gael's hard work—the hard work of the whole team, really—it became open all year.

Gloria Barrett

In the beginning, people were very suspicious. They thought they were all grass-smoking hippie-dippies; tree huggers. A lot of people didn't use the place. That was difficult. But the ferry drivers were very positively affected because, during the night, when they docked on this side for fifteen minutes, they would run up to the bakery, get a bun. I was the only one there; there was no one on cash. "Just put the money somewhere."

Little by little, in terms of this community, the action really started for Gael, for the bakery, when the "implants" came and the part-timers, the holiday people. A lot of the people who were the best customers, from where I stood, were the visitors who came—the people who had houses here—from the US and from Ontario and so on. They were here for maybe two weeks of every year but, boy, they were supportive. They were there lining up. It was great. And a lot of people from Bridgewater used to come out. I think, for the most part, what people were really grateful for was that the old building was taken care of. That was a big one. And now you could get food and you didn't have to go to Bridgewater every time you turned around. It changed the way of life in LaHave, for sure. And it got more and more that way and it's excellently more than that way now. I mean, she's got all the food, the dinners, the veggies, the groceries. Hallelujah!

Andra White

I know at the beginning a lot of the locals called it a hippie place and they wouldn't come and shop here. As time went on, Gael would see some of the elders, some of the locals, coming in. It meant so much to her to win the support of the locals. That was really important to her.

SEVEN DAYS A WEEK

Kathryn Gordon

Gael really had to struggle through those early years of the bakery. She tried all kinds of things. At first, she kept the bakery open seven days a week. Then she started closing on certain days. But hearing reports that people would drive all the way down to the bakery and it was closed, she had to bite the bullet and keep it open every day. At many times of the year the business lost money, but she kept her staff employed. She found ways through wholesale to keep it running, and then she would be in the black by the end of the summer.

Gael Watson

Very early on, I realized that we needed to be open every single day, seven days a week, twelve months of the year. In the winters, in order to make sure people still had work, we started making jams and jellies. At first it was very little. I think the first thing we made was the marmalade, Donald Robertson's Seville Marmalade—my father's recipe. We started with that one because Seville oranges are harvested in January, February—our slowest time of the year. We would get cases of them. This led to making other things in the slow time of the year, and that's been the way the bakery has held on. We just switch gears in the winter and start manufacturing things.

HUSTLE BUSTLE

Gael Watson

Rhonda McKearney and I were the first bakers. Within two weeks of opening, I hired another five people to work at the bakery, so it went from two of us to seven of us. I was the bread baker, the main baker. I was baking the whole time. I also delivered the bread.

Gloria Barrett started working at the bakery that first fall as a shopkeeper. Fran Aldercott was a shopkeeper, too. Gloria was also the one who would come in at three o'clock in the morning. I'd finish baking at three or four. Gloria would come in. She bagged and labelled the bread, and packed it into various crates and boxes. And the baskets. We used Stanley Corkum's handmade witherod baskets. I would be napping; I had to have a two-hour nap before delivering the bread.

By 1992, Kathy Fisher, who was from LaHave, came to work at the bakery. She was in charge of the lunch counter. We served sandwiches and pizzas—the little pizzas. The lunch counter became quite a big part of the bakery.

The accounting office for the LaHave Outfitting Company, which was at the front of the building, was initially my office. Then it became a curio shop for a couple of years, where Wick—Robert Wikstrom—sold earrings and other pieces of jewellery on consignment. After the curio craft shop left, we put tables in there for people to sit at.

We did a Sunday brunch, which was fun and also very successful; very well attended. We always did eggs Benedict, and we had omelets and waffles or crepes, pancakes, scrambled eggs, often French toast. They were delicious!

Gloria Barrett

We, all of us, pretty much did everything there was to do. No specialty trades. We used to really clip along! I kind of designed a job myself after Gael got the wholesale business going, which was really good—saved our bacon in a lot of ways. The bread was baked. By midnight the bakers would be finished, and they'd go. About one o'clock, when the bread was cool, I would let myself in and I'd do what I had to do, which was to pack up the wholesale orders. Gael had a huge list of wholesale orders. Halifax, originally, and Liverpool, Port Medway, and all around the town. So that's what I did. I bagged the bread, I priced the bread, I labelled the bread, I packed the bread, and put it somewhere where the driver would get it in the morning. So it was perfect, really. I worked in silence. I said to Gael, "I love this job. I love what I'm doing." And I was there for twenty-one years. I left when I was sixty-three.

The work at night was good for me, personally, wonderful, because when I went to work, everybody was gone. The doors were locked, the phone never rang, and I would do my job. I remember it took me five and a half hours to do all those wholesale orders. I'd take a break about three o'clock in the morning and go out on the dock with my tea and my dog. I mean, it was heaven; it was bliss. I should have been paying Gael.

The girls would work downstairs in the bakery and bring big baskets of bagels and pitas and cheese rolls and things like that up to the main floor where I was working at that time, years ago. It just became impossible to walk around and find a place for my bread orders and all that stuff, so I just pushed the baskets a few inches out onto the porch at the front. One night, a skunk came down the road and helped himself to a bagel. And I thought, "I'm not going to confront a skunk. Take the whole basket!" One of the girls came up with another full basket. She saw the skunk and dropped the basket, and everything went all over the place. She must have thought, "Oh my God, we're going to stink the

Bakers in the LaHave Bakery bread kitchen. From left, Connie Hyson and Debbie Bagnald, c. 1992. (UNKNOWN)

place up. It's all over," and she flew back down the stairs. Anyway, the skunk was very much more interested in the bread he was eating. Looking back on these things, you think, "Yikes!"

Sometimes, at night, my hours crossed over with the bakers. It was interesting; they all had their stories, just amazing stories of resilience. Sometimes, bakers needed to bring their children to work with them. You'd go in there, you'd see a child asleep on the bags of flour—wonderful, soft, really good bed—right out of its little baby mind, while its mother baked the bread.

LIVE AND LEARN

Gael Watson

The intensity of the beginnings of it. I remember the squeeze of having to make it work. When you don't have a lot of money to throw at something, you are faced with either admitting defeat or thinking through the night about what you could do to alter the situation. The brain, under pressure, is an incredible mechanism. Something will pop up: "What about this, what about that, what about...?" Possibilities open up and you try something. You can have failures, but really, they're only lessons.

I was completely dedicated to paying my bills. If you ask somebody to do something for your project, you are, at the same time, making a commitment. Whatever it takes, you're going to make sure that person is paid for their contribution.

I'll tell you a story. It was the first week at the bakery, and things had gone well. I was impressed. People coming in the door, saying, "This is really neat," and, "What an amazing old building," and "What good bread this is." At the end of the week, when the shop closed, we were all chatting together. There were seven of us. Everybody was in a good mood, laughing and talking about the customers, and so on. Then I said, "Would you mind waiting another week for me to pay you?" All of a sudden, there was silence. Silence in the room. And I understood. All these people had helped me, and it was my thing, this bakery. They worked hard all week, and I had no right to ask them to wait. I left, and the very next morning I went into Bridgewater to that place where you can get short term loans for an exorbitant amount of money. It was 48 percent interest or something like that, but I borrowed the money in order to pay them.

From that day onward, I understood that it wasn't just the staff. I couldn't call a plumber or an electrician or a carpenter, I couldn't ask for supplies from a distributor, unless I was prepared to do the work to make the money to pay them. I think that very basic thing has made the years go from one to the next. We survive because the bills are paid. Very simple: you've got to pay the people who have done the work. You also pay your bills for your own sense of preservation, of who you are and what you're doing. I was raised to be responsible for myself and what I do. When you sign your name on the dotted line, you're in. That commitment to pay the bills pushed and expanded the bakery's business. Taking the bread into the city and into various markets, selling it, was how the bread became known, how people got to know it existed.

Very early on, there was an older Dutch couple, Dick and Marie Smits, who were really keen and positive and supportive of the idea of doing a bakery in LaHave. They originally ran the bakery at the IGA in Bridgewater, and then they had their own bakery called the Dutch Oven, in Chester. Really nice couple. Dick Smits was an inventor, and he built a big, stainless steel ice cream machine to make hard ice cream. After their bakery closed, I bought his machine. I was really intrigued so, for a couple of years, I made ice cream. But I was making it with cream. It was very, very rich, and, at that time, in the late '80s, people were against butter; they were against cream; they were against whole food. It was all about light, spelled "l-i-t-e." My ice cream just wasn't very popular. Even if I made the smallest batch, I could never sell most of it. I could never sell half of it. It was just an expensive thing that I wasn't making money with, so I had to give it up.

Gloria Barrett

Gael was good at thinking of ways to save money, which, of course, is a must. She started getting butter in a block about the size of a toilet, this jeezly big thing. I could see her behind the counter with a sharp knife trying to get everything segmented. I thought, "This is not going to work." I mean, you get a dollar off this block of butter and then you spent $20 hiring somebody just to cut the Jesus thing. But, you know, she said, "Live and learn."

Gael Watson

In 1991, we opened a LaHave Bakery outlet in Mahone Bay. A lot of stuff was baked there in the early years. Eventually, very little got baked there. We kept it going as an outlet for twenty-eight years.

I thought that a third retail outlet would bring more money in. I was able to rent what used to be the tiny Post Office in Italy Cross, right on the 103 Highway. We made nice wooden shelves. It sold bread and sweets and jams. Antonia McGuane was the main shopkeeper, and she did a great job. It was a sweet little outlet. My thinking was, "There's a lot of traffic on the 103; everyone is on the 103, this is good." Wrong! There is a lot of traffic but it's moving too fast, and it's dangerous. Driving to drop off the bread order, I would look in my rear-view mirror and, if there was a transport truck coming along at 120 km/h, I didn't chance it that he might not see me. I had this terror of being run over by a big truck, smeared by a big truck. So I thought, "Well, if I'm doing this, I'm sure lots of people are." Good idea but wrong location. We closed it up after about four years, in 1995.

The LaHave Bakery outlet in Mahone Bay, 2007. (JANE MORRIGAN)

Peggy Greer

The bakery had Thursday night dinners for the community. A lovely lady named Sharon Riley worked with Gael and me, and the three of us created a menu each week. We offered two sittings with twenty-five or thirty people at each one. It was wonderful fun. We made great food, all in that tiny kitchen, and people loved it. After a while we realized that, by the time we made the meal, served the meal, cleaned up after the meal, and planned for the next week, we wouldn't get home until eleven or eleven-thirty. Clearly it was too much for all of us, but especially Gael. It was back to "I'll sleep every forty-eight hours."

Gael Watson

The Thursday night dinners were something. We had choices—vegetarian and meat. There was usually a theme; we would do a Greek meal or a French meal, an Italian meal, and they were very successful. We did them for about three years, through the winters. After a while, I began to find it hard to go home to a cold house at midnight, and so I was really the one who said, "That's enough for now."

FIGURING IT OUT

Gloria Barrett

In the beginning, Gael was just doing everything that her sensibilities dictated. She would go through the fog, doing the thing, making decisions, looking after two kids, starting a new business, and she was stellar. She really was.

Gael Watson

I was doing the calculations, and the question was, "How do I bring in enough money to pay my loans?" Not so much what do I need to produce, but what do I need to sell in order to get this money? It had to be quite a lot. Not only that, but I had to take it out, wholesale the bread, so that it could sell. I very quickly realized it couldn't be a one-person bakery like I was doing at home.

Kathryn Gordon

Gael is good at business. If she's going down one path and comes across an obstacle—like when she was having a hard time finding organic flour. I think a mill where she was getting her flour had closed. And so she took the time—and I don't even know how she had the time to do everything she did—but she found somebody to grow the wheat. She found somebody with a stone mill. Suddenly that flour was available to her again.

Those are roads that most business people wouldn't take. They would maybe accept what was and maybe go with the next easy thing, and probably the cheapest thing. Gael is definitely really smart about pricing, too. She knew where to cut corners, and where she wasn't willing to cut corners. And she was never willing to cut corners when it came to the quality of the product. She's a determined woman; she's very headstrong and she gets things done.

Gloria Barrett

You'd have to be half crazy to do something like Gael did. You know what I mean? Because who would take on a building like that? But my God, she just had such vision. I always called her a visionary. There was one summer she hired two big guys who moved massive beams underneath that building to keep it from being claimed by the ocean, the river—whatever. They were worth their weight in gold. It was wonderful to see, and it made all the difference, but Gael saw all that. She saw what needed to be done, so it all started to take shape. It was like a phoenix, rising out of the ashes. This part got done, then that part got done. She got the building back.

Gael Watson

"Wick" [Robert Wikstrom] was a prolific artist; a man who could make a living in Petite Rivière in those years from his own work. It took a lot of ingenuity, and everything was original. He had so many different things for sale, and they were all priced to sell. He never put things out of range of an ordinary person wanting to buy something. I took that as a really good lesson: "Don't overprice, don't think your stuff is worth so much that nobody can afford to buy it."

That really made sense to me. Gloria Barrett does that with her paintings, too. She wants people to have them, and she's been able to work as an artist, as a painter, most of her life in LaHave.

TREE OF LIFE

Gael Watson

The wharf, by the time we bought the building, had gone—washed out to sea. I agreed that it was important to have a wharf. It was around 1990 when Covey Island Boatworks in Petite Rivière was asked to build a large schooner called the *Tree of Life* for Kelly Kellogg. They were in the beginning stages of building the boat and needed a place where it could be finished. A wharf was needed.

Mike personally took it on. He was going to build that wharf so that this roughly 70-foot boat could be finished here at LaHave Outfitters. Mike built the wharf with hemlock beams—big beams. He and Ronny Reinhardt built cribs on the land. Brady Himmelman, who was known for being the skipper of the LaHave ferry, had a large four-wheel drive tractor with a front-end loader.

Construction of new wharf at the building, with Brady Himmelman operating the tractor to launch one of the cribs, c. 1990. (UNKNOWN)

When each crib was built, each large crib, Brady Himmelman would come and push it into the water. It would sink and then get filled with rocks. There were three pieces of it, and that's how Mike built the wharf in time for 1991, when the *Tree of Life* was launched at the ferry wharf in LaHave and towed to the new wharf at the bakery.

The end of our building was made into a workshop where they did all the finishing, all the rigging, all the building of the beautiful cabinets and hatch covers; all of that was built here. The *Tree of Life* was the impetus to get the wharf rebuilt. It did last, considering how much abuse the ocean storms bring in. It has been repaired over the years. When you have a building on the water, you want access to the sea, and that was a really important thing to Mike. I agreed. And I still feel it's important, having that access to the sea.

Peggy Greer

The nautical aspect is a big part of the place. Mike played a huge part in restoring the building, of course, and also building the wharf and turning the waterfront into a marina. When Covey Island Boatworks moved from Covey Island to Petite Rivière, the bakery was very important. There was room in the upstairs of the bakery for storage, and once the boat was in the water, all the work could be done right there. It became the in-water worksite for the Boatworks.

Tree of Life *tied up at the LaHave Bakery wharf following the ship's launch at the LaHave ferry ramp, 1991.* (UNKNOWN)

Gael Watson

The *Tree of Life* was the first boat that was tied to the wharf to be finished at the bakery. Kevin Wambach had a boat shop at the back of the building for many years. He, as well as other people who worked for Covey Island Boatworks, would work in that shop on all the boats that had been launched. All the finishing work, all the beautiful woodwork and spars. The *Tree of Life* was the first, followed by many, many other launches. We would get to know the people who planned to spend time on their boats. That was nice. That went on for quite a few years—a decade, at least. So the wharf was used, and the floating docks were used, and there were parties with the launchings that went along with that.

Sadie Watson

The *Tree of Life* was an amazing boat that Covey Island Boatworks built. Kelly Kellogg, the owner, bought a house just across the street from the bakery. He brought family and crew to finish the boat. A lot of them were teenagers. For me, the openness, being able to spend time on the boat and spend time in that house and get to know these Americans, was very influential.

CHAPTER 4

Rising Above the Ordinary

BREADS

Gael Watson

THE BREADS I STARTED WITH WERE THE BREADS THAT I WAS ALREADY MAKING AT home before we bought the LaHave Outfitters building. I made different things out of what I got from the garden. I liked the idea. I was making potato bread because I had potatoes. The first breads were Milk and Honey, Potato Bread, Swedish Limpa, and Oatmeal Molasses Honey. They were recipes I got out of local cookbooks, and then I adapted them.

Those were the early breads, but then things happened. Somebody would bring something in, and we would make a bread with that, or somebody had an idea, and I would think, "That's a good idea," and try that out. An example is Gloria Barrett. She lived in Réunion, in the Indian Ocean, for several winter seasons. She would bring back bags of black pepper—all these different varieties. So I made a black pepper bread, rolled in crushed black pepper—pepper and parsley. A lot of parsley. We'd make parsley bread. Some of the breads were very seasonal.

What a small business can do is listen. Many of the things I've done at the bakery have been because people have told me about things. Some of the bread is glazed differently, according to what people ask for. It doesn't have to be my way. I'll do it my way, but it doesn't have to be totally created by me. If somebody has a good idea and they're not a baker, but they'll eat the bread, then I'm going to make that bread. It makes sense. Because I was baking a lot in those early years, I was always making up new recipes. That's why we've got around forty-five different kinds of bread. It would be boring to make the same kind of bread every day.

I had a very old photograph of the LaHave Outfitting Company. It wasn't very clear, kind of muddy, but it's what they used for their label. I took it to a friend of mine, Mary Troyer, an artist, and asked her if she could do a line drawing from that photograph. She did, and that's the logo for the LaHave Bakery. The script used on the logo is from Marnie Troyer, Mary's niece, who still to this day will make up signs for us with her beautiful scripts. I asked her if she would do the bread labels with the logo, so she did all the labels, initially by hand. Since then, we use the computer to copy them.

WHOLE INGREDIENTS

Gael Watson

Even before the bakery, I used whole ingredients instead of the dried, processed ingredients, because dried, processed ingredients had allowable additives. When the bakery started, I decided that I was going to make the bread as clean and true to its ingredient list as possible. In 1983, I got a booklet out of the travelling library, the Bookmobile, and it was called *The Truth About Food Additives*. It was a publication that two Canadian women put together. It was wonderful; really informative about additives that are in common foods. I was extremely influenced by it. The pamphlet was later published as a book called *Hard to Swallow: The Truth About Food Additives*. It was shocking how many known carcinogens there were, there are, in some additives. Since they are used in trace amounts, they don't have to be listed as ingredients. So beware! Anything you buy that is processed may have those things in it.

Most people are used to soft bread. They will take a loaf of bread and squeeze it to decide whether they're going to buy it or not. Well, our bread, within twenty-four hours, is getting hard. That's what bread does when it doesn't have additives in it. It deteriorates over a short period of time, which is why we say, "Keep it in the fridge." It's a perishable food.

I say, "Question any food that isn't breaking down." If you have something on your shelf for six months and it hasn't shown any signs of breaking down naturally, and you choose to eat it, chances are it's going to have a negative effect on you, sooner or later. It's going to catch up with you. It's true that some people can eat processed foods all their lives and live to be 105. They've got the bodies. They can handle it. They're tough. A lot of people aren't so tough, and they succumb to these things.

When we were living in the apartment at the bakery, I had this loaf of "100 percent whole wheat" commercial bread. I put it on the top shelf of the cupboard in the kitchen and every week I checked it. It was always the same. You could still squeeze it. It looked the same; no mould, absolutely the same loaf of bread sitting there. Weeks and weeks passed. It was sometime over three months when I checked it again and it was "fine." The very next day, it was gone. It was like magic. It had become this grey dust inside the bag. I thought, "That's convinced me."

It was very groundbreaking for me to realize that the only real control you have over the food you make is by getting unprocessed ingredients and knowing every step. Like in the case of the wheat, I know the person growing it, I know their philosophy, I know their practices. I can, on behalf of my customers, confidently buy this wheat, and make it into food that is unadulterated.

You need to be curious and ask questions. You can't look the other way when it comes to food. You can never get it 100 percent, but whatever you can do, it will be better.

☙ ❧

I had lots of people coming when I started the bakery, saying, "I'm at your service." One of them was Pest Control. He said, "We're going to keep the insects and the rodents under control here." I'd seen the truck everywhere. All the grocery stores had that truck sitting outside.

I said, "Well, I've got bags of flour here and I'd have to move them all out before you spray."

Him: "Oh no, I can spray all around it."

Me: "What if the bag's been sitting there for three months? It's going to get inside the bag."

Him: "Uh, no."

That was another eye-widening moment of realization. I saw that truck everywhere, every convenience store, every restaurant, knowing that there he was—pshhhhhhhhh—spraying pesticide. That led to me thinking, "Oh my god, the mills; the warehouses." So an ingredient is in a country far away, and it's in a warehouse and it's sprayed. Then it goes into a ship that has been sprayed, and then it goes into a warehouse over here, and that's sprayed. If it takes a year, or if it takes four months, it's been sprayed many times. You can almost count on it, that pesticide has made its way into the food.

WHOLESALING

Gael Watson

The first season, 1985, was going well. Then Labour Day came, and there was almost nobody around. There wasn't enough to pay the bills. So I got a booth at the Halifax Brewery Farmers Market. I would bake the bread, Gloria would pack it while I was napping, I'd get up about five in the morning, pack Sadie in her car seat, and we'd head to Halifax. The bread sold really well at the Brewery Market, but I didn't sell all of it. I'd go from there to a flea market in Dartmouth and sell more bread. Then, if there was still bread left over—because the rule in my mind was: "You're not going home until you sell it all"—I would take the remaining bread to various stores and wholesale it. There was a store called The Little General on Spring Garden Road in Halifax, and then there was The Big General [on South Street]. That's how the wholesale business began.

On principle, I wholesaled to small, independently owned stores in the beginning. But I needed to have more sales; it wasn't enough. Also, there was a problem with some of the smaller stores. They couldn't make a go of it, and they didn't pay me. So I went to the big stores, to Superstore and to Sobeys, and set up accounts with them. As it is right now, there's about five or six very small accounts, in private enterprises, and then a number of Sobeys stores and some Superstores.

I had friendships with a lot of the people I wholesaled to over the years. Tom Rousell, who owned Soho Kitchen in Halifax, used to buy the bread. He would come out occasionally to the bakery to visit—a really nice man. It became a wider community, rather than just always staying in LaHave, and it brought people to the bakery.

THROUGH THICK AND THIN

Gael Watson

I would do the deliveries. Twice a week to Halifax; once a week to a few places in the Annapolis Valley, and once a week going south, to the west, as far as White Point Beach. There was a little grocery store at the time in Broad Cove, and a couple of places in Liverpool.

I'd pick up the unbleached white flour from Dover Mills, and any other things I needed in Halifax, and then return. In *all* weather. I was determined, if the bread had been baked, it was going to be delivered. In all the worst weather, in vehicles that didn't have proper snow tires. There were a few times when we would get stranded on the side of the highway. I'd have to change tires in the winter on the side of the highway. Things like that. And then, back home, and do it again.

I was the one baking the bread and I was the one delivering the bread for quite a few years. When Mike came back from sea, he did some of the deliveries. Then, a number of different people delivered the bread after the first seven or eight years of my doing it. The wholesale trade was a necessity because it did two things: I was able to sell more bread, and people got to know the bread. They saw the label, and that helped.

One day, I was delivering bread in a little Toyota truck. There was me, Sadie in the car seat, and Jesse next to her. Jesse was about nine, and Sadie about three years old. It was winter. We'd finished delivering in Lunenburg, and the witherod baskets were all piled in the back of the truck. We were on our way home when suddenly I noticed that the children didn't have their seatbelts on. I barked at Jesse to put Sadie's seat belt on, because the roads were slippery. He put her seatbelt on and locked himself in. We went around the next corner, and there, sliding towards us, was an oil truck. I couldn't get out of its way, so I drove off the road and the truck tumbled. We ended up upside down, all of us hanging like possums in the truck, and the truck was completely smashed. We could see, upside down, the driver of the oil truck running toward us. I could tell he was terrified he'd just killed us. He ran over and down into the ditch, and opened the truck door. He released Jesse first, and Jesse fell into his arms. I'll never forget because Jesse, at that age, was so embarrassed to be carried like that.

He got us out and we were fine. He called the tow truck, and the tow truck pulled this crushed vehicle out, and the witherod baskets had survived in the back. They'd been rolled over, the truck had rolled over them, and they survived.

Anyway, what are we going to do? It's our only vehicle, it's winter, it's getting dark. I got in and turned the ignition and it worked. I got the children back in the crushed cab of this crumpled truck, and we drove, all squished up, to Normie Veinot's, which is near Pleasantville. All the way there, Sadie was saying "Don't cwash Gael. Don't cwash!"

We got to Normie Veinot's. The next delivery was three days away. I said to him, "I will pay you $1,000 if you will fix this vehicle in two days—get it going again." It might not have been $1,000, but whatever it was, it was a large amount of money because I needed that vehicle for delivering the bread. It was enough for Normie to take it on. He worked day and night, straight through. Nobody believed that we'd been in an accident, because the vehicle was in perfect condition. He'd hammered it all out and smoothed it, lots of body filler, and away you go. Looking back on it, it was an indication of how I just had to keep those wheels turning. I couldn't let anything stop. It *had* to be done. The bread had to be baked in all kinds of weather. In those days, every day, every moment, every possibility, every cent that could be made had to be made, and often with the children in tow.

Later, for many years, we used a courier to make the bread deliveries. There had been incidents, either with drivers, or vehicles not being in good shape. It was too much of a risk. At first, couriers gave me really good deals, but then it became too expensive, so we returned to delivering the bread ourselves. By having our own van again, we often drop bread off at someone's house if it's a good order, like seven or eight loaves, and if they are not too far out of our way. Or we meet people in a parking lot. Cellphones are good for that: "I'll meet you somewhere." We do lots of rendezvous, picking up supplies for the bakery while we're on the road.

NOVA SCOTIA-GROWN WHEAT

Gael Watson

The idea of growing wheat for the bakery came from my sister, Jane Morrigan. In her enthusiasm, she said, "I could grow the wheat for you." So that began at my sister's dairy farm, Morrigan Jerseys, in Pictou County, Nova Scotia, in 1986. Jane grew organic hard spring wheat for the bakery. It was really important to me that the wheat was grown in Nova Scotia, and that my sister was growing it.

Jane Morrigan's wheat being harvested in Pictou County for the LaHave Bakery, 1990. (JANE MORRIGAN)

I bought a little stone mill to grind the wheat into flour. It was about a 15-pound mill, with a tiny stone turner. It had a huge hopper on it, so I wasn't running up and down the stairs every ten minutes. The problem came when Jane had to wait in line each year for the combine. The wheat couldn't be harvested right on the dot, right at the perfect moment. This caused the wheat to lose a certain amount of its protein content. I found that I couldn't make 100 percent whole wheat flour because it wasn't strong enough. That, in turn, made me change the recipes so that there was always enough unbleached white flour to mix in with the wheat flour. After three years, Jane and I decided it wasn't practical to keep doing it.

I went from Jane's wheat to buying organic stone-ground whole wheat flour from Speerville Mill Co-op in Speerville, New Brunswick. Stu Fleischhaker, manager of the co-op, would drop in from time to time. He was always fun to deal with and he could answer questions about how the crop was doing; keep me updated. It was a good relationship.

Meanwhile, I was approached by Jock Peill, a very nice man, who grew wheat and had a big stone-ground flour mill at his farm, Lyndhurst Farms, in Canning, Nova Scotia. His mill was about ten feet by ten feet, as opposed to my little mill that was ten inches by ten inches. He was very persuasive. He really wooed the bakery to buy his wheat flour. And I did, because it was local, it was Nova Scotian; that was better. So I went from Pictou County to, briefly, near Fredericton, New Brunswick, then back to Nova Scotian wheat and I was really happy with that. I had quite a few years with Lyndhurst Farms, up until Jock died. So that came to an end, and I went back to Speerville Mill in New Brunswick. By that time, Stu Fleischhaker had retired, and I really missed him as manager.

At that time, the market was driving wheat prices way up, even though there wasn't a shortage. Suddenly, a fifteen-dollar, 20-kilo bag of wheat flour almost doubled in price. I thought, "I can't depend on that." I realized how vulnerable we are when we have to bring stuff in from the rest of the country. So then it became a real campaign about getting wheat from Nova Scotia.

I made a lot of calls to a lot of farmers, always asking for hard spring wheat. I put the phone down after the last possibility fell through and I thought, "Wait a minute, it doesn't need to be spring wheat, it could be winter wheat, if winter wheat is easier to grow." Once I started asking, "How about winter wheat?" there was a person, Jeff McMahon of Longspell Point Farm, in Kingsport, Nova Scotia, who said, "Sure, I'll try it."

To encourage that possibility, I said, "If you're successful, I'll buy every bit of it. I will buy however many tons you end up with." And I think it was around eight or nine tons that he got out of it that first year, and I bought it all.

There was a man named Peter Fuchs who had a mill near Peggys Cove, Nova Scotia. We partnered in milling winter wheat produced by Jeff McMahon. I bought one little mill and he had a little mill, and between these two little stone mills, Peter was grinding all the 100 percent whole wheat flour for the bakery.

BUYING LOCAL

Gael Watson

I think there is a way a manufacturer, small as we are, can work with farmers. With Jeff McMahon and the wheat, I wasn't financing it, but I was promising—I was guaranteeing I would buy it all. I think that's a way people can work together. You can negotiate in small ways with small growers and small manufacturers. You're completely out of the loop with big business. You're not allowed in. You can't negotiate. You can't say, "Well, if you do this, I'll do that," and it's no fun. When you have a conundrum, you get around it by being flexible in the way you think. And, of course, that's way more interesting.

Peggy Greer

Local food was hard to source initially, but Gael would do the research, the digging, the driving to contact farmers throughout the province to purchase organic grain, meat, and dairy products. She would go to the farms to meet the farmers and make sure that everything was to her liking. She wanted to know where the food came from, what it was, how it was made.

Gael Watson

Gennoe's Baking Supplies in Stellarton, Nova Scotia—suppliers of raisins and currents and all our chocolate chips and everything—have been supplying the bakery from the beginning. The company used to be known as BMS Distributors. Knowing them over all these years, the people at the desk, they're nice people; you get to be comfortable. So many of the people we deal with, we get to know.

John Sampson, Captain John Sampson, from the Magdalen Islands, had a farm in Italy Cross. He walked in the door of the bakery one day, and said, "You can buy my honey." So I did, buying it from him for years.

Peter Fuchs also had a small-scale oil mill he was using to press local organic canola. He would deliver the fresh stone-ground flour and canola oil to the bakery. Because I was a very small business, the oil he made was enough for the bakery.

There was a man named Stanley Corkum who made witherod baskets. He would sell some of them to the Gray brothers when they owned the LaHave Outfitting Company. After we bought the building, we made an arrangement with Stanley to continue buying his baskets. He was eighty years old at that time, and he brought those baskets to us every year for another twelve years or so. And I bought every single one. Everything that he brought in his car, I bought. We used those wonderful handmade baskets, and we still use them to this day. We carry our bagels and cheese rolls in them; they're really tough baskets. Stanley Corkum lived to be 106 years old. Making witherod baskets was a skill that his father had shown him, and his father before.

SLEEPLESS IN LAHAVE

Kathryn Gordon

Another memory I have is the first winter after the bakery opened and Mike went to sea. Gael worked so much, around the clock. She had bunk beds constructed outside her office so she could be there with the kids and bake at all hours. Jesse was eight and Sadie was two at the time. The office was where the kitchen is now, and the bunk beds were in what is now the dishwashing room. Gael would sometimes be so cold she would have multiple sweaters on and two hot water bottles—one on her lap and the other at her feet. It seemed right out of a Charles Dickens book to see Gael in her office, paying bills, surrounded by dark wood, old safes, and pressed tin ceilings. A wonderful image!

Gael Watson

We were asked by Chris Huntington and his wife, Charlotte, to do catering at properties where large auction sales were being held. In those very early years, we were desperately in need of money, so of course I said yes. The catering—the killer catering. I would bake all through the night. We made all these things like Scotch eggs, chicken turnovers, sausage rolls. An array of finger foods. We'd also have various drinks—lemonade and coffee and tea.

Peggy Greer

Mike worked at sea in those early years of the bakery. Gael worked so hard she was only sleeping every forty-eight hours. She would work non-stop for two days at a stretch, doing pretty well everything. Then she would sleep a bit. She would forget to eat. There were times she would come to my kitchen and I would say, "When was the last time you ate?" And she would say, "I don't remember." At that point, I would stand in front of the door and tell her she wasn't allowed to leave until I fed her. Those days were hectic and a bit frightening, but I admired her. She worked so hard. It was all-consuming. She was baking, selling, and delivering the bread by herself, living in that big building with her two kids.

CHAPTER 5

Extraordinary Times

STAYING AFLOAT

Gael Watson

MARY BAWDEN WAS FROM MASSACHUSETTS, AND SHE WAS A LOVELY PERSON. SHE bought a house on Bell Island. She supported the bakery. She was fun and optimistic and positive. She would come and stay for the summer. One night, after she had returned home to the States, she phoned me. I was in this regimen of sleeping, maybe, if I could, two hours a night, from 3:00 A.M. to 5:00 A.M.—the time between the end of the bake and when I had to start deliveries. She called me in the middle of this precious sleep—sleep that would determine whether or not I could make it through the next day without collapsing. She said, "What are you doing up there? How is it going?" In my exhaustion, I said to her, "I don't know Mary. I may not even be here when you return." I hung up on her. I was mad.

The next day, Jean Gaudet, the bank manager from the Royal Bank walked across the road and sat down on the black bench and sipped at his coffee. I came in to say hello. He said, "I had a phone call from Mary Bawden this morning."

I said, "Oh, yeah! Gee. She woke me up. I need my sleep." I was very cranky with the bank manager. He listened to me quietly. Let me come to a fizzling stop.

He said, "Well, she's asked me to set up a joint bank account for her and you. And she's put $2,000 in it for you to use, because she felt that you might need some help."

I stared at him. I didn't say anything, but I thought to myself, meanly, "She's rich, she should give me more!! Two thousand dollars, that can't possibly help me out! I owe thousands and thousands of dollars!" I just walked away from him, into the office, and I broke down and cried. Finally, my tiredness and frustration spent, I realized that I had $2,000 more than I had five minutes ago, and that I was going to make that work. I was going to get through the winter. I was going to sip it, slowly. For every little bill that I couldn't quite make, I would use this money. I made it through because of that $2,000, and I learned a very important lesson that I would have missed if she'd given me more. Mary Bawden had given me the most wonderful, amazing gift.

The early years were very hair-raising because there was never enough money. It was my responsibility to pay the bills. Nevertheless, we kept slipping and slipping behind in the years right up to the late nineties. It was touch and go. One day, a scout, a film scout, came by and said that a Disney production was interested in using the bakery shop in early June for three or four days. I had, just prior to him coming in, established the fact that if I couldn't find a way to get $8,000, we were doomed. That happened from time to time. "We're doomed if we can't get this money!" There was always a way to figure out how to get that money, or hold somebody off for another four hours—"I'll have it here by this afternoon."

The bank was calling me every day telling me I was in overdraft, and so I was making these promises every day. It was very stressful. Eight thousand dollars is what I needed, and in walks this guy named Shaun telling me that Disney Productions would like to rent the space. I said, "Well, that's high season. That's when we make money. So it's going to cost you, because I need the amount of money that I would normally make, and I'm going to make that money anyway. So I need $8,000." He said, "$8,000!!! There's no way. That's ridiculous. We don't pay that much money." I just shrugged my shoulders and said, "That's okay." He said, "Well, let's go for a drive." He had a little sports car. I got in the sports car, and we drove along the road to Crescent Beach. Nice guy. He rolled a joint and passed it to me and we smoked it. When we got back to the bakery, he said, "I'll get back to you tomorrow, whether or not we can do this." The next day he came and he cut me a cheque for $8,000 and saved the bakery. I always say, "Walt Disney saved the bakery!"

The Disney movie set that was staged in the LaHave Bakery shop, c. 2000. (UNKNOWN)

I'm remembering one time there was an auction in Middle LaHave, and it was a great auction—lots of people, did very well. Very well. At the end, we packed up everything into the back of the truck. I was so exhausted that, instead of going back to the bakery to unload, I just drove home. I came in the door and shoved this bundle of money under the sink and tucked it in behind the pipes. And there is where it stayed until one day, ten years later, I got a call from the bank asking for money. I said, "By the end of the week," and they said, "No, tomorrow. You have to come up with this money tomorrow," and it was something like $2,000.

I came home. I was crying, "How am I going to do this?" For some reason, I went under the sink to get something, and I was low enough that I looked up and there was this envelope. I pulled it out, and even as I pulled it out, I knew, "Oh, my god," the realization that I'd never even missed it for ten years. It was close to $2,000—the exact amount that the bank needed the next day.

FOR THE BIRDS

Gael Watson

Right in the very beginning, one of the reasons that I didn't want to leave our home was that I had my hens and my duck. When Mike came back from sea he said, "You know, it would be a whole lot easier if we were to move into the apartment in the building." But my hens; my duck—I couldn't part with them. At that time, the end of the building was still very rough, so we moved the hens into a room there, on the second floor, overlooking the river. That's where the hens lived, in a coop. So from the very beginning, there have been birds in that room, but at first they were laying hens.

Jesse Watson

Gael and Mike made a chicken coop at the back of the building. That was kind of different. "What were we going to do?" We couldn't leave the hens back at home, so we brought them to the building. I remember taking food and water to them, tending and checking them.

Gael Watson

One day, Mike brought a small parrot home from the pet store in the Bridgewater Mall. It was a red lory. His name was Eric, and he was such a character. He lived in a room in the apartment, but he had the freedom to come out of it. We had a big, long table and he would use it as a landing strip. He'd fly down and he would go, "Eyu, eyu, eyu" across the table and do hilarious things like dump his head into a glass of milk and then shake it, or dump his whole face into mashed potatoes. He loved mashed potatoes. He was just hilarious, and we have wonderful memories of him. For some reason, we thought it would be fun for Eric to be in the shop, in what is now the lunchroom, because he didn't have much company upstairs during the day. We had a tree on a stand that we put in there, and that's where Eric was. He was a pretty good bird. For the most part he stayed in that room, in that tree.

It all ended, very abruptly, the fun of having Eric in that room. He was always like a crow, always very interested in sparkly things. One day, there was this fairly large woman who had a lot of jewellery around her neck, and she had a great, open cleavage. Eric looked across and it was like his eyes rolled. It was so magnificent, this view of the woman with the huge cleavage and the beautiful jewels dripping down in between her breasts, and it was too much. He flew over and dove his head right down into her cleavage so that only his legs were sticking out! And then, the woman just screamed and someone said, "Quick!" Mike rushed in and actually had to put his hand down into her cleavage to get this bird out. We thought better of putting Eric in the shop after that.

GROWING UP IN THE BAKERY

Gael Watson

Sadie has really, even in utero, been connected to the building. It wasn't until the winter of 1984 that we actually bought it, and at that point she was one year old. When the bakery started in July 1985, Sadie was a year and a half. How she survived is a miracle to me because it was such a blur of activity. The animals were still back at the house, twenty minutes away. Sometimes, I would start the bread with a cold mix to slow it down so that I would have time to go home to feed the animals and stay for a while. Then I'd go back to the building to continue baking through the night. Using cold water was the trick. In the winter, I would walk down the long lane, often with Sadie on my back, to feed the animals and load the woodstoves.

Gloria Barrett

Gael's kids were with her all the time, of course. They were too little to leave back at the house. Sadie was sweet. We all loved her. She had twenty-five mothers. Everybody was going to Frenchys [a used clothing outlet] and getting her little rigs and stuff. Very, very sweet. And somebody taught her how to use the washing machine. They pushed a little bench up against the machine and told her what the buttons were and showed her how to do it. She did her own laundry. She was four or something.

Gael Watson

There were what we called the "flour bag children." Sadie would often settle in amongst the bags of flour to sleep while I was baking. Just a good baby, and cheerful. Fortunately, right from the beginning, Sadie has been her own person, very social. She was interested; a good listener. Those early first customers took a liking to her. My friends Peggy and Marion would come and pick her up and take her for outings. Peggy had many children, including Zoe, who is Sadie's age, and they played together. Mostly, Sadie played in and around the building. She was always able to amuse herself.

Once, when I left the safe open downstairs, she went into it and selected some of my jewellery—the most sparkly of all. She went out towards Ruby's house, to the stone wall, and made houses in the rocks, decorating them with these jewels. I don't know how long my jewellery was down there. One day, I went to get Sadie. She showed me her little houses, her little dolls, and little furniture that she had made from driftwood and rocks and various other things she'd found on the beach. My eyes lit on the jewellery. Unfortunately for Sadie, it had to go back into the safe.

Gloria Barrett

Gael and the family moved to the upstairs of the bakery, into what is now the apartment they rent out. I remember Sadie was two and a half inches high. I used to cook. All I knew how to cook was curry, so I cooked the curry and walked down the road with it from my house to the apartment. We'd sit around that big table up there, and Sadie's feet didn't even touch the floor. I remember sitting there, time after time, with dear little Sadie, and the curry was hot because I didn't know how to make it not hot. Sadie was there with her little feet dangling, and she would take a mouthful and she would go, "Whoo-whew, whoo-whew, whoo-whew." She did that the whole meal, and she finished her plate. What a sport, you know. Those are the things I remember so fondly.

Sadie Watson

I basically grew up in the business and in the building. I was born at the end of '83, and the bakery opened in '85. So I was pretty little. I remember being raised by a lot of women and by the community. Someone was always keeping an eye, but I was pretty free-range. Ruby and Lawrence Gray, next door, used to take me in for spans of time. That's where I got my *Sesame Street* and my grilled cheese sandwiches. In the building itself, it was busy; really busy in the summer. I would go with Gael to run deliveries all over western Nova Scotia. Sometimes when she worked late, I'd be sleeping on flour bags with my little quilt, or I'd be napping. I still remember being bathed in the big double sink when I was little. Stealing raisins out of raisin-orange dough. I was forbidden to steal the raisins, but I would—they were so tasty. I remember my eyes would just come up in line with the counter and I'd pick the raisins off, and then I'd run away. The dough that came with the raisins would rise in my stomach and I'd end up feeling really sick. I'd lay on the black bench in front of the shop, and everybody would scold me for eating the raisins.

We'd sled down the hill across from the shop, hang our wet clothing on the big radiator in the shopfront, and then help ourselves to the sweets and hot chocolate and litres of milk. It was a very free-range upbringing. I think, at the time, I felt like I was on my own, in my world. In retrospect, there were so many people around that there was always oversight. Growing up in that way was a unique experience.

I almost burned the building down once. That was bad. I was four or five years old at the time. I had these fairy houses and forests on the beach, all around the building, and in the building. I thought that I'd planned everything out. I had two buckets of water, and I had my fort. "Oh, if the fire gets out of control, I've got water, and I can put it out." But for some reason, there were straw bales around the propane tanks that were quite close to my fort, and the fire quickly got out of control and lit around the propane tanks. David Himmelman, who owns the fish plant and larger boats next door, came running. I, fortunately, didn't run away and hide. I was screaming, "Fire!" and "Help!" so people immediately came. Gael and Mike evacuated the bakery because there were bakers working and propane ovens running. Mike got the hose out, and then David Himmelman came over with the big hose from the fish plant and got it out. I remember being mortified, because I'd taken all the precautions, and yet I almost burned it all down. It could have been the second big fire in LaHave since 1957. So that wasn't good.

My work at the bakery started when I was little. Gael would put me up on a five-gallon bucket and I would be boiling bagels. I remember that very specifically: a big pan of boiling water. Gael would be shaping them and shifting them over onto pans and I would pick them up and drop them in boiling water. When they puffed up, I would take the scoop, scoop them out, put them on the next pan, and then I'd do the sesame seeds. That was a very formative memory.

I also learned how to use the scale when I was very little. I would chop and weigh the dough. I was always given jobs that I could do. When Gloria was packing bread, I would put the labels in. I probably knew all the breads, all the loaves of bread. And then bagging the bread. All those jobs that children can do.

I really started working at the bakery when I was eleven or twelve, working full summers. I would be making cookies—hundreds and hundreds and hundreds of cookies for the cookie jar. And working the shop. That bridged into me working the cash. It was good. It was fun. Hot! Really busy; insanely busy. The scale was different. It wasn't as busy as it is now, but we had fewer people working. I learned how to work as part of a team long before high school; long before university. It was choreography, really. You had to get that choreography right, working the shop, or things would fall apart. You get hungry people who were just upon you. We were bagging the bread for the shop. The wholesale stuff was all done by Gloria or somebody else. We were cutting the sweets, keeping the sweets case full. On the lunch side, making sandwiches. At that point, we didn't have a separate kitchen. We were doing it all out in front, in the shop, most of it. Doing the dishes. Just getting it done, but it was also a lot of fun because you were working with your friends. It was good. It was a way to make money and pay for a car and pay for plane tickets, for Frenchys binging.

Gael Watson

Sadie was there during all kinds of situations with customers and with the people who worked there. From a very early age, she was helping. She was always helping. Of course, when she was little, in order to help, she had to stand on things. So there was the long counter in the shop where there'd be a bucket or an overturned box. Those were the places where she would stand to cordially look after the customers. She could use the cash register at a very early age. Downstairs in the bakery, she would boil the bagels for us, again standing on an overturned bucket. When she grew older, closer to twelve, thirteen, fourteen, fifteen years of age, she was working in the shop. She knew the answer to just about any question that any customer ever asked. She was on top of it, and in full control. Really, she was liked by all, and so I hope growing up with the bakery has been mostly a good experience for her.

RUBY AND LAWRENCE

Gael Watson

Living next door to the LaHave Outfitting Company building were Lawrence and Ruby Gray. They were probably in their seventies, in '84. Lawrence was a member of the Gray family who owned the building before we bought it. Right from the get-go they were warm and interested, supportive and helpful. They were wonderful neighbours; truly encouraging.

Jesse Watson

I remember spending time with Ruby and Lawrence Gray in their little house next door, yarning with them and hanging out. Lawrence would be puttering in the yard, and he'd either call me over or I'd go over and visit with him. He'd come out and chat people up along the side of the building, continuing to do what he'd done all the years before with his brothers and his dad when they owned the building. In hindsight, I feel pretty lucky that I knew Ruby and Lawrence. I also remember Teleen and Gala Gray, who lived in the apartment before us. I remember going up there. Pretty early memories also of going across the road to Gala's garden, where she'd be in the thick of it, doing her thing, gardening up there.

Gael Watson

In those early years, when Sadie was very young, Ruby really looked after her and looked out for her quite a bit. Ruby and Lawrence didn't have children of their own. They were very kind, like grandparents. If I was wondering, "Where is Sadie?" I'd look next door, and if I saw her tricycle parked outside, I

ABOVE: *Ruby Gray and Gael Watson at the LaHave Bakery, c. 2015.* (JANE MORRIGAN)

BELOW: *Lawrence Gray in the accounting office of the Lahave Outfitting Company, c. 1978.* (PETER BARSS)

knew she was there. She'd go into their house and kick off her boots, and Ruby would make her a cheese sandwich. Sadie would sit on a stool at the counter and eat it. Lawrence would turn the television set on in the other room, so Sadie would be able to watch *Sesame Street*. That was something. They were very good neighbours. I would often go over at some point in the day and sit in the rocking chair in the kitchen. Ruby's mother, Vera, who was in her late nineties, was living with them at the time. Another elder for Sadie to look to. She had only one eye. She had lost the other eye at some early point in her life, so it was closed over. One day, when Sadie and I were driving, she turned to me and said, "Why does Ruby's mother have only one eye?" And, before I could come up with an explanation, she said, "Oh, I know; when you get to be that old, you only need one eye."

Sadie Watson

Ruby and Lawrence shared what they had. There wasn't hesitation, never "I'm too busy," it was just "Come on in." It was molasses cookies and grilled cheese sandwiches. They had CBC on their television. My only time watching *Sesame Street* would've been at their house. Lawrence would come in and have a yarn. He would sit in his chair. Everything was very consistent, in a very comforting and reliable way. That is who they were for the community, and who they were for us as a family. They were very supportive; I remember that.

TEMPEST WINDS

Jesse Watson

I remember when the new roof blew off in 1987. I was sleeping in the front corner room of the apartment. I was dreaming that it was really stormy, and a building I had made out of blocks was being knocked down, was crumbling. In the middle of this dream, I was woken up by Gael. "We gotta get out of here!" I woke up to this full-on storm, of course influencing my dream. I was getting things together quickly, getting dressed, getting shoes on or whatever, and going to use the bathroom. Opening the bathroom door, the gyprock and inside trim opened, just like a mouth. It was crazy. All this snow blowing in, swirling in the bathroom. You could see outside, then the roof would slam shut. It was surreal.

We made our way down into the basement and hid out with Gloria, who had been packing the bread. The power was out. There were sparks and stuff coming off the power lines, and things falling. It was dramatic. The next morning, we were walking around and surveying the damage. Posts were down around the cars and everything. We were looking up—"Where did the roofing go? Where's the metal?" This was heavy gauge metal, too, not like that flimsy stuff now that you can bend just transporting it. We were looking down the river, thinking maybe these big pieces of metal blew off like leaves and had sunk. I remember I propped up a ladder, climbed up, and looked, before anyone. I saw that all the metal was still up on the roof but crumpled up. It looked like crumpled up newspaper. So that was the answer. That was pretty crazy.

Gloria Barrett

One night, there was this fierce wind. It blew a window out upstairs, close to where I used to work—one of the big windows. But, as luck would have it, we were all safe and nobody got hurt. But the building had its own life. We really intruded upon it because it had been fallow, so to speak, for a lot of years and then suddenly there was all this activity and renovating going on.

Sadie Watson

Being here when the big storms rolled through was such a wild experience. The building is one-third built over the water, so whenever a hurricane came through, it was always exciting. There were boats and floating docks breaking free, windows blowing out in the building. It's made me ready for changing conditions and changes in people, in the environment, in the weather. I feel I'm always ready for whatever is coming. And it is probably because I grew up here, in the bakery. It's a big aspect of how I navigate my life as an adult now.

CHAPTER 6

The Bakery Boat

THE *SELCHIE*

Gael Watson

A BIG BOAT IS SOMETHING THAT MIKE REALLY WANTED. HIS PLAN WAS TO DO THE old trade route between Nova Scotia and the Caribbean. Ten years after the LaHave Bakery opened in 1985, we found an old scallop dragger—a wooden scallop dragger that was built in 1962—from Meteghan, Nova Scotia. This was the one that would do it. We were able to purchase it. It was certainly floating, but it was in rough shape. Needed a lot of work before it would be in a condition to go south.

Her name was the *Lady Denise*. We couldn't keep the name because they were building a new one, so we had to come up with another name. I named the boat the *Selchie*. A selchie is a mythical creature that is a seal in the water—in the sea—which can transform into a human at night. A selchie's true home is the ocean and, on the land, the selchie always mourns for it. That's why it's very important never to capture a selchie in its human form—because it will only pine for its lost life in the ocean.

The first trip, bringing the boat to LaHave, to the bakery, was very adventurous. From Meteghan, we had to go around by Yarmouth and then Shelburne and keep going to the east. The former owner had painted the deck, so it was slick, and there were no bulwarks. We ran into a storm. We put a line between the bridge and the bow of the boat. It was quite a high line. You had to hold onto that line, and that was how we precariously moved around. The boat was pitching in the sea, and everything was being tossed down below. At one point, I decided that I would go from the fo'c'sle in the bow toward the bridge. I was going with the line, hand over hand, when the boat suddenly pitched and I flew into the air, holding onto this line. I swung, back and forth and back, not being able to get my footing because it was slippery. Finally I got my footing and carried on.

Babe was with us. She was our dog, and she loved going on the *Seal*, the little boat that we had before the *Selchie*. So she was all for it when she went with us on this trip, but, as I say, it was rock 'n' roll, and dangerous. When she got off that boat after that first trip, she never went on another boat again, that dog. Babe, the dog. I asked for forgiveness, but she shook her head; no way she would ever go on that boat again. She walked down the road to Gloria and became her dog. Gloria packed the bread at that time at the bakery, and Babe would keep her company. Babe understood that she had a choice. She made it really clear she was not going on the ocean again. That was that.

Babe was very well known. Gloria painted her several times—wonderful paintings of Babe. She was a very exceptional dog. One day, I had a basket full of baguettes. Babe decided she was going to offer one to Gloria, so she carefully took it out of the basket and walked straight down the road with this fresh baguette and handed it to her. Gloria did a painting of Babe with the baguette. We still have that painting. For many years it was at Mahone Bay, but now it's back at the bakery in LaHave.

LAHAVE MARINE BAKERY

Gael Watson

Unfortunately, the *Selchie* would take quite a bit of fixing up before it could leave the shore. Therein, there was a dilemma: "How do we come up with more money so that the boat can be fixed up?" Standing upstairs in the gallery, looking out at the boat, I said, "Well, why don't we put a bakery on the boat?" It was really still the only thing—the only way that I knew I could contribute to getting enough money to fix up the boat. It was a novel idea, and so we prepared the boat. It had to be ready to be a bakery by the first of June.

There was a lot of work done. We gutted the officers' quarters. The *Selchie* was ninety-six feet long and twenty-four feet wide. She was a beamy boat and had an old-fashioned carvel-planked wooden hull, but was powered with a 500-hp Caterpillar diesel engine. Mike put a lot of energy into getting the boat gutted. We had people that volunteered to help. Two people who came along to help were Jeff and Jackie Amos. When we bought the boat, it didn't have bulwarks, so we put about fifty spruce tree "knees" on to support the new bulwarks. We got the *Selchie* to the point, that first summer of 1995, where we could take her around Nova Scotia, the mainland of Nova Scotia. I wanted it to be called the LaHave Marine Bakery, similar to the way that I wanted the bakery to be called the LaHave Bakery. I had a large sign made that was attached on the wall below the bridge and above the kitchen. It wasn't just a floating bakery to me. We were out on the ocean.

The first year, we rented a 50-kilowatt genset, a large generator from Caterpillar, because I had two ovens and a 20-quart Hobart mixer. It was a really nicely designed galley. There was a carpenter in Bridgewater who made cabinets, and he made the pantry cabinet for me. I designed it with pull-out bins, and you could push the bins back in and lock them in place so that they wouldn't swing out and break your legs at sea. It was the perfect little galley, about twenty feet long and nine feet wide. Because it was a working boat and we'd be selling food to the public, it needed a sticker on the window, an approved health permit sticker, so it was licensed. It was a licensed galley, a legal working boat. I was very proud of that. And it meant we could buy fuel at a greatly reduced price. Being able to buy diesel at the cheap price, the same as the fishermen, that really made it possible to actually consider that it could make money.

Gloria Barrett

Well, it was such a brilliant idea. I did a little painting and they hung it in the galley. But the thing was, Gael was up and down those gangway stairs or whatever the hell they call them with flour, with bakes. Honest to God. But it was a great idea. It was well loved and brilliant, just brilliant.

Peggy Greer

The bakery boat was not a boat. Let's face it. It was a ship, and it was huge. So sailing it, living aboard it, going to communities, baking all night, sailing on

Mike Watson and Gael Watson standing in front of the Selchie *in dry dock at Lunenburg Foundry, 1996.* (GLORIA BARRETT)

to the next community, meant Gael was once again on the non-sleeping, non-eating, twenty-four-hour scary treadmill. It was wonderful for the communities they went to, and it was a wonderful thing to do, but it was frightening for me to watch. I know what it's like working on a boat. It's tough. The boat throws you around all the time. I've cooked on the open sea plenty of times, but to do all that with no time to rest, it's too much. When I said to Gael, "You've got to stop this," I meant it.

AT SEA

Gael Watson

We'd start to prepare in May and run through until the end of October. It was three six-month seasons.

There was a time when, off Louisbourg, I was having a nap down in my cabin, and I suddenly woke up to the sound of silence. Silence on a boat that is only powered by a diesel engine is not a good thing when you're offshore. I jumped out of my berth and ran up to the bridge to see what was going on. There were just three of us on the boat that time. The engine had cut out, so I took the helm while Mike and Sylvain went down into the engine room to see what the problem was. Mike ran back up the stairs to say, "Serious problems." The fuel line had come apart from the engine, but was still pumping diesel. So this snake was going all over the place, and covering the engine room and this huge, huge Caterpillar diesel engine with oil. It was pumping the oil out. He ran back down again, and I was on the radio letting people know we had no power. It was so hot down there, you couldn't breathe in it—the heat and the fumes, the burning in your eyes, the smoke. But somehow or other, between those two men, they lassoed that line and got it reattached and the engine started up again. That was a close call, because we were quite close to land. Fortunately, the tide was going out, so we were drifting away from the shore instead of into the shore. If the tide had been going in, that would really have been curtains. Anyway, all was fine, no harm done, and we continued on.

On that trip, we passed by Saint-Pierre and Miquelon, the French islands, and after we passed them, we saw a lot of birds in the sky. Then we realized they were circling around whales, humpback whales, breaching. Huge, huge, huge. I mean, always, whenever I've seen whales, it makes life worth living. You can be really sad and then it changes completely when you see whales. There's something about those magnificent mammals that takes you right out of yourself and your little worries about what's going on in the world. The whales, everything evaporates with the sight of them.

We went around the outside of Cape Breton, which was really magnificent. We went to Souris, PEI. We went to New Brunswick, into the Richibucto River, and down to Shediac. We went to Newfoundland. We went to all kinds of places along our route. Several times to Pictou, Nova Scotia. I have great pictures of the rising loaves of bread, the porthole behind, and a beautiful, beautiful morning, and smokestacks spewing from the pulp plant. I was always struck by the breathtakingly spectacular geography of Pictou Harbour. And then there was that plant spewing filth.

BAKING ON THE BOAT

Gael Watson

I was the main baker, but each year we had help. One person would be at the door selling the squares and cakes and breads and sausage rolls and cinnamon rolls, and there was one person washing dishes. All of us on the boat would share the responsibility, at sea, of taking three-hour watches. We would pull into a port at night, usually, and put our little sandwich board on the wharf, saying that we would be open with fresh-baked goods at eight o'clock. And, amazingly enough, there would be people that would come down. Sometimes it would be advertised—not that we were advertising, but there would be articles in newspapers. That's how people would know about it. I would get up at three thirty, quarter to four, start the genset, and then go down into the hold and bring up bags of flour and pails of molasses, whatever I needed for the bake. I started with the bread and, because there was limited space in there, I had hooks in the ceiling where the buckets of rising dough would hang. Once all the bread was started, I would move on to squares and cupcakes and dozens and dozens of cinnamon rolls. They were popular. Also, sausage rolls. The sausages came from The Pork Shop in Denmark, Nova Scotia. They were very popular, too.

Usually I was baking once we were stationary, but sometimes, when the conditions were right, I was baking as we cruised along. We went through St. Peters canal in Cape Breton, Nova Scotia, into the Bras d'Or lakes. The lakes were very calm so that was one time I could bake as we went. The pails would gently sway as we cruised along. It was very idyllic. I remember going through the dark blue Bras d'Or lakes with a lot of pleasure because it was so very beautiful. The smell of the baking bread. At one point, I made a batch of cookies for us all. We sat out on the hatch cover of the deck to have tea while we cruised along, going up and into Baddeck, up to the wharf. We went to Baddeck three times. The last year, 1997, we were there at the same time as the Tall Ships, and *Matthew*, the reproduction of John Cabot's boat. There were Tall Ships on the Bras d'Or lakes. At one point, we got close enough to throw loaves of bread to a passing Tall Ship. That was kind of fun. The hours would go; it was seven days a week. Sometimes we would be in a port for two days, very rarely three, and mostly only one. We'd come in at night, spend the day there, then leave again at night, and then on the seas again.

I never had any problems with bread rising on the boat. It probably was a nice environment for it. Sometimes it was quite cold; the breeze, the coolness of the ocean was coming in on the bread. People would wonder if that was good for it. But it was fine. It turned out quite nicely. I'd sell it for two dollars a loaf, and I'd make about seven or eight different kinds. They were baguette-style loaves.

AT THE WHARF

Gael Watson

One time when we went into Canso, Nova Scotia, a 104-year-old woman came on board. That was pretty wonderful. She had lived there all her life. She came across the gangplank, and she was really cheerful and wiry. It was so nice that she enjoyed coming on the boat.

In our third year, 1997, we went to Newfoundland. It was the year of the Tall Ships, and we were alongside them on several occasions. We went up to Bonavista and into that small harbour with them. There were smaller harbours, too, that we'd pull into. I'd get going, baking alone when it was still dark. I always had a pot of coffee on. Retired fishermen would come down, would see the light at the wharf, and they'd come on board and ask, "What's up?" I'd offer coffee. They'd settle down and tell me stories about fishing in the old days.

The stories the old fishermen told were mostly about the loss of the fishery—how it had happened so quickly. They would say that the fishery needs to stop for twenty years to give the landscape of the ocean floor a chance to recover. And they were pretty adamant about that. It made perfect sense. Leave it alone for twenty years. If you're going to have a moratorium, make it across the board; don't let anybody fish for twenty years. But that never happened and, of course, we're still in a crisis.

Women would come on board, and we'd talk recipes. They would ask about making different things like muffins. In Newfoundland, they called them "moof-fins." "Have you ever made partridge-berry mooffins?" If there was something in particular that they wanted, something they grew up with, I would try my hand at it and say to come back later. Based on their description, I would make up a recipe. It was fun to do, and they appreciated that I was making an effort. Sometimes they would bring things, let's say black currant jelly, and I'd make black currant jelly-filled donuts. That was very popular, jelly-filled donuts on a boat.

On June 29, 1997, the *St. John's Evening Telegram* had the *Selchie*, the bakery boat, on the front page. We shared the front page with the Queen, who was visiting Newfoundland at the same time. You know, the Queen and Newfoundland. That was pretty wonderful! Of all the places we visited, St. John's, Newfoundland, was the busiest. Nobody had a problem crossing the gangplank into the boat, marching on board. Standing room only, all over the deck and up around the bridge. At one point there were so many people on one side of the boat it suddenly listed to the port side, and everything in the galley went sliding!

MISSING DOG IN NEWFOUNDLAND

Gael Watson

Of course, there was also the big event in St. John's: our dog, Storm, went missing. We had gone up to eat in a restaurant, leaving Storm in the bridge, the only place that could be locked. Suddenly, we heard, "Boom!" Fireworks going off. Knowing that Storm was terrified of thunder, we both jumped up and ran out of the restaurant, all the way down the streets towards the harbour, towards the dock. But it was too late. Storm, in his panic and fear, had thrown himself against the bulkhead door until he broke the latch.

This poster was distributed all around St. John's, NL, by Roan Haysom when Gael and Mike's dog, Storm, went missing, c. 1997. (JANE MORRIGAN)

There were people who had seen him running. One man said, "Yes, yes, I saw the little dog, and he ran right between my legs, right between my legs! And he went off in that direction." I was very upset. He didn't come back that day or the next day. I think we were there about five days.

Our good friends Valerie Hearder and her son, Roan, very nicely photocopied pictures of Storm and stapled them to telephone poles and electric poles. Storm was everywhere. He was a familiar face.

I found it really hard to bake. It was very, very popular, very busy. I was baking from four in the morning to ten at night, every night that we were there. But all the time there was the absence of Storm. The radio station came and so did the television station. They wanted to do a story about the boat. I took advantage of the opportunity, and said, "I will, but I'm missing my dog, and this is a picture of him. I want you to put him on TV. I want him to be on the radio."

"Ooohh." They went away saying that they would talk to their bosses about it. They came back and said, "Yes, we'll do that." Fortunately, that was what saved Storm. He was found with bleeding paws by a group of people, five miles away. There's no way we would ever have got him back if it hadn't been for, "Have you found your little dog? I'm praying, we're praying for him." It was just so sad.

In the interim of him being away and lost, there was a cat that came on board and slept on Storm's bed. When Storm came back, as he did, and he was filmed reuniting with us, the cat disappeared. The cat kept his bed warm.

On the very last day, when the Tall Ships had moved on and we were still there, another wonderful thing happened. It was sunny and warm—this beautiful, warm day—and Storm was back and everything was good. Life was good again. Valerie, her daughter, Leitha, and son, Roan, came down to the boat with a big picnic basket. They shook out a blue checked tablecloth and put it over the hatch cover. Then they pulled out this cold bottle of wine, wine glasses, and this wonderful array of food. I will never forget it, that kindness. For years, when I would talk about that, it would make me cry. It really meant a lot to me. It was this moment in time that stood still.

MEANWHILE, BACK IN LAHAVE

Gael Watson

While we were at sea, I was away from my post at the LaHave Bakery. The bakery continued working seven days a week, and I had also, a couple of years before, started another bakery in Mahone Bay. Fortunately, the invention of the fax machine and the cellphone meant I could keep in contact with the bakery. Cellphones were like shoe phones—the size of a shoe. Whenever there

Gael Watson on the bridge of the Selchie, *ordering provisions for LaHave, Mahone Bay, and the LaHave Marine bakeries, c. 1997.* (UNKNOWN)

was reception, I would contact the bakery in LaHave and they would contact the bakery in Mahone Bay. Both of them would fax me forms that they'd fill out in the morning and the evening. I would get the information about what they needed for supplies and anything that was happening that I could respond to. They would also let me know their hours because I calculated the payroll. All the ordering for LaHave and Mahone Bay was done from the boat. I also ordered for the boat and had to know when I would be in a certain place so the truck could meet me with the supplies. That's how it worked.

Whenever there was a problem at the bakery, I found it really hard to get my head around the fact that it was real. When you're on a boat, on the ocean, the land doesn't exist for you; it's just an afterthought. I'll never forget not being able to believe that there was land. I would be informed that there was a problem with the plumbing or the oven or something, and I had to go along with it in a sort of make-believe way. It had to do with the way my mind was working at sea. It's the swell, the motion, the feel of it. You're just 100 percent on the ocean, floating on the top, the vastness of it, and so totally dependent on that boat to keep you alive.

Kathy Fisher was the one who really kept the wheels turning at the LaHave Bakery for those three years we were at sea. She did refuse to keep Storm for us, though. At first, we were going to be leaving him behind and that was going to be one of her duties. We had gone to Shelburne with the *Selchie* and were dropping into LaHave before we continued on our journey. Kathy marched Storm out to the boat and said, "There's no way I'm keeping this dog. He's trouble." And I knew she was right. He was just so much trouble, making a nuisance of himself wherever he'd go. But he was really comical; a great dog.

One time in Lunenburg, in his exuberance, Storm leapt off the tall forepeak of the boat down onto the dock before we even reached it. Another time, late at night, on one of our many visits to Lunenburg, Storm was nowhere to be found. I stood on the dock, listening to what I thought was the sound of mussels opening as the tide dropped. But when I looked down between the boat and the dock, I saw Storm's little face just above the water, and his feet clawing desperately to keep him afloat. I yelled for Mike, and as I pushed the boat away from the dock he climbed down the side of the boat and rescued him—just in time. Storm could climb the companionway ladder, no problem. A dog that can climb a ladder is a useful dog on the sea. He would go out onto the very bow, almost to where the bowsprit was, and lean out to sea as we cruised along. Completely confident; complete balance as he leaned out over the bow of the boat, his ears flapping.

We did that for three years. Three seasons. Miraculously, the bakery boat did make enough money. It paid for itself. Not a lot, but it did make money and it did mean that it could be fixed up further, with a mast. It was beautiful when it left LaHave in 1998. There were a lot of things done to it, a marine-band radio went on, and a ten-person life raft. That raft ultimately saved the lives of all on board when it sank two years later, off Honduras. That was the end of the *Selchie*.

PART 3

Momentum

CHAPTER 7

Bread

COMFORT AND COOKSTOVES

Gael Watson

MY GRANDMOTHER WAS A REALLY GOOD BAKER. MY EARLIEST MEMORIES, EVEN before I was five years old, come from the comfort of the smell of her baking. Still, absolutely to this day, I tie in my comfort with the smell of baking. I love it, and it's a passion.

Living in our homemade house without power, and being a tea drinker, I always kept the stove going. For all my waking hours the cookstove was going so I could have a kettle boiling. If you want to have a kettle boiling, you've got to have a hot enough fire, which gives you a hot enough oven for baking. The loneliness I felt during those years, and the soothing memories of the smell of baking from my childhood, influenced me to bake bread—and usually more than we could eat. Hence, the day arrived when somebody was interested in buying my bread. Her name was Gwen Kavanaugh. She was my first customer, long before the bakery opened.

AVOIDING ADDITIVES

Gael Watson

Ingredients are one thing and additives are another. Additives are all about shelf life for processed foods. It's very difficult to avoid buying food that does not have additives. Health Canada considers that approved additives in trace amounts will not adversely affect your health. They don't even have to be listed as an ingredient. I had thought that the law required every ingredient to be listed. This was a real eye-opener for me.

If you're consuming foods that contain trace amounts of additives every day and your body doesn't recognize them as food—as something it can utilize—it will store them in the fat. Also, the natural composition of some foods has been altered, their structure changed, either through processing or through hybridizing, and the body may not recognize them either. As I see it, it's the accumulating additives that cause people to have allergies and side effects that they can never figure out.

Table salt has additives in it. Garlic salt, garlic powder, onion powder, powdered egg yolks, and a lot of those sorts of things have additives in them to keep them from caking. They're there, but they're not listed.

Then there's flour. There are many different kinds of flour you can buy. In some flours, there are additives called dough conditioners, and they are enzymes. Those enzymes can be natural or chemically formulated. They promote a large, soft loaf of bread. A natural bread is soft the first day, then by the end of that day it's getting harder. It gradually dries out until, by the fifth day, it's really getting stale. That's because it's real food.

There are somewhere between fifteen and twenty-five different additives that can go into all-purpose flour. That's why I chose unbleached flour, because there's no additives except for the enriching ingredients, like iron and B vitamins. I can't buy unbleached flour without them. That's a questionable thing too, "What are the sources of the enriching ingredients?" When wheat is milled to make white flour, the germ and bran parts of the grain are separated from the endosperm, which is the white part. White flour doesn't have the roughage of the bran, or the disease-preventing nutrients of the germ. So, by law, flour manufacturers have to add enriching ingredients to white flour to put back some of the nutrients they removed.

Wheat has gotten a bad rap. A lot of people don't eat wheat. I think a lot of it is because of what's been added to the flour. It's not the wheat. Wheat has been eaten for thousands of years, successfully. We could probably look at a lot of foods that have become something that people can't eat anymore, and it's not the original substance that's to blame, it's the changes—the alterations to it.

MILLING WHEAT AT THE BAKERY

Gael Watson

When Peter Fuchs gave up milling wheat, I found another miller. The new miller did it for a while, and he did a good job. But he was charging me more for milling the wheat than Jeff McMahon was charging me for growing, harvesting, cleaning, drying, and storing it. It didn't seem fair that the farmer would get less than the miller. That was what made me change it up. I said, "I'm getting a mill!"

I found one that's made in the States, and I really like it. It's a good mill, a very basic machine. It's bigger than the initial one I had years ago—three times bigger—and it does a beautiful job, stone milling the wheat into flour. It keeps pace with our needs.

It was very exciting, thinking about where to put the mill. I thought about it a lot. It would be a problem, definitely, for people to be breathing that dust from the flour. So where was I going to put it? Was it going to be separate? Was it going to be in my house?

No. There was that room with the engine in it, the old Fairbanks-Morris diesel compressor that used to power four freezer rooms for fish. We had been thinking about the fishery: "Let's have a fishing museum." Jesse took on cleaning the engine, then we cleaned up the room. So I was eyeing that room.

That's where I was going to put this mill. It wasn't going to be a museum. We put a partition in the room with glass, so you can look into it in that old-fashioned way. And it's a great thing. The mill room is also used as the storage room for almost all the dry goods that we sell at the bakery. And from the grocery store, you can see into the mill room.

STONE-GROUND WHEAT FLOUR

Gael Watson

Stone-ground wheat—the definition is the entire wheat kernel, ground up finely, and made into flour using stones. The stones move a lot slower than a steel mill. Therefore, there is less heat. So the best flour is stone-ground because nothing is missing; none of the elements are destroyed by heat.

A schooner and crew alongside the LaHave Outfitting Company wharf, c. 1920. Across the water is Riverport, NS. (Unknown)

The LaHave Outfitting Company delivery truck, c. 1937. The painting on the side reads: "LaHave on the Label means Good Fish on the Table." (Unknown)

The LaHave Outfitting Company building at the time of purchase in December 1984. Jesse Watson is in blue; Mike Watson in red. (LEIGH ROBERTSON)

In December 1984, the LaHave Outfitting Company building was falling into the LaHave River with the weight of the iron refrigeration pipes. (Leigh Robertson)

TOP: *Gael Watson loading her Volvo with bread in preparation for wholesale deliveries, c. December 1985.* (Unknown)

BOTTOM: *The LaHave Bakery and wharf viewed from the LaHave River, c. 1996.* (Unknown)

FACING TOP: *Customers in the LaHave Bakery shop, c. 2016.* (Jane Morrigan)

FACING BOTTOM: *Map showing the locations of some of LaHave Bakery's suppliers, c. 2021.* (Artwork Anna Bald, photo Jim Bell)

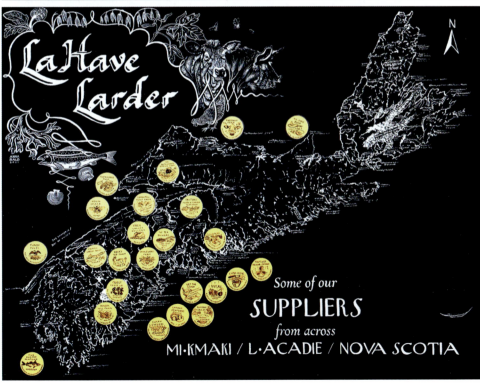

The LaHave Marine Bakery serving customers at a wharf in Nova Scotia, c. 1996. (Unknown)

Breads and sweets on display in the LaHave Bakery, c. 2017. (Jane Morrigan)

Cooler filled with locally sourced and other fresh produce, 2021. (JANE MORRIGAN)

The LaHave Craft Co-op, c. 2000. From left, Gael Watson, Gloria Barrett, Kathryn Gordon, and Duff White. (ANDRA WHITE)

Jesse Watson of Homegrown Skateboards with his "Home" boards stacked to sell, c. 2000. The codfish graphic on this deck was designed by Selwyn Sharples. (UNKNOWN)

My mill has two vertical stones that grind together. There's a hopper on top of the mill that you pour grain into. You turn the mill on and open the hopper. The hopper shakes the grains, "Tshh-tshh-tshh-tshh," down into the stones. The stones are turning and grinding, pulverizing the grain. Then the whole wheat flour comes down through the bottom of the mill. It looks really nice coming down into the pail. And you can tighten the stones—you can tighten or loosen them. If you want to have cracked wheat, then you open the stones up. If you want flour, you close them down.

STEEL-GROUND WHEAT FLOUR

Gael Watson

Steel-ground wheat is taking that wheat kernel and putting it through steel rollers. Steel is faster and hotter, so right off the bat there are certain nutrients in the wheat that are being destroyed. It also separates the three major elements of the wheat kernel: the bran, the germ, and the endosperm.

It was explained to me by Dover Mills many years ago, that steel-ground "whole wheat" flour is white flour, unbleached white flour, with some bran put back in. Unless it says stone-ground, it's steel-ground. A great big sign on a loaf of bread saying it's "100 percent whole wheat," misleads people. Steel-ground whole wheat flour doesn't use the entire grain. It's got the germ missing. The most important, vital part of the grain is not in it. So—hoodwinked.

Most commercial bread is made with steel-ground wheat. But it doesn't have everything that's in a kernel of wheat. White bread flour only has the endosperm, the white part of the kernel. It's missing the fundamental parts, the bran and the germ. The germ is very perishable. They remove it so flour and bread can have a longer shelf life. It keeps longer because the best part, the germ, is taken out.

ENRICHED WITH WHOLE FOOD

Gael Watson

Bread is basically made of flour, water, and yeast. Basic bread has just those three ingredients. My bread has more. It started with living down on our land. I was growing vegetables, making bread on a daily basis, and incorporating what I was growing into the bread. So my bread is more than flour, water, and yeast.

The flour is important. The flour and the liquid are about equal parts, and they make up the largest part of the bread. I use unbleached white flour so there is no bromate, there are no additives at all other than the enriching ingredients. At the LaHave Bakery, we use more unbleached white flour than whole wheat. But all the whole wheat that we do use, in bread, squares, oatcakes, and other things, is coming from Nova Scotia, and is ground fresh using our own stone mill.

The liquid in bread is a big ingredient, almost half. It can be many different things. It can be just plain water. An advantage of being in LaHave is that I have my own deep well. It's clean water that does not have chlorine in it and doesn't require chlorine. When you think about it, any food that is made in a commercial setting, like in a city or a town, the water has chlorine in it. So a lot of food has chlorine in it. Our food doesn't. I think that's meaningful.

Most of the breads have a little honey, not necessarily made sweet, but yeast wants a little bit of sweetness as food. Rather than putting sugar in it, we use honey. I made a choice in the very beginning to use honey instead of sugar in my bread, and I continue to use honey because it is full of nutrients.

All the bread we make has a little oil in it. The reason you put oil in it is to help make the bread more tender. I always put a little bit of oil in every batch.

Because the unbleached white flour we use doesn't have the germ and the bran in it, we add in our own natural enriching ingredients like eggs and milk. If we make an herb bread, we use onions. We peel onions and we peel garlic, and we blend them with herbs. A loaf of potato bread has potatoes that we peel and boil and mash and add to the mix. I never use dried milk because there are anti-caking agents in a lot of dried ingredients. I don't use dried onions or dried garlic or dried eggs. Our white bread is enriched with food.

Then, of course, the whole wheat breads are made with the entire wheat that we grind, so we know it's the entire grain. The entire grain is ground every day and mixed into the bread. There's nothing taken away from it, and the germ is in it. They're pretty healthy breads. You could live a long time on a loaf of seed bread. It's 65, 70 percent whole grain—whole wheat mixed with seeds and some of the unbleached white flour, so it's not so dense and heavy.

The bread has got a lot of food in it. I like the idea of bread being food. Our bread is like produce. It goes bad as fast as produce does. If you want to keep it for a long time, think of it as fresh produce. It should be refrigerated because, at room temperature, it will soon break down—as it should.

JELLY BEANS

Gael Watson

The LaHave Bakery is a wheat bakery because we can grow wheat in Nova Scotia. We can't grow rice. Wheat is what's available to me. I don't have to worry if a truck can't come in. I can drive over to the Valley and get it.

Years ago, people started asking for gluten-free. "Got anything gluten-free?" I saw there was a market, and I was encouraged by other people to take advantage of this. I thought, "Maybe I'll try it, but I'll do it myself." For about two or three months, I was making bread with ingredients that were just totally foreign to me. Corn starch and rice flours and different flours from different countries, and guar gum and xanthan gum. It was a weird feeling, standing in front of the mixer putting these things in.

But the bread turned out to look like bread. I mean, it could be bread. It certainly had that look about it, even though it didn't smell right. I was going along with it until, one day, I was mixing this concoction and somebody came down the stairs and said, "The phone is for you." When I got back, I looked down into the bowl. It had become a bowl of jelly beans! I turned the mixer off, turned the speed up, and started it again. It went, "Pa-ba-ba-ba-ba-ba-ba," trying to pound the jelly beans into a mass that I could make into bread. There was nothing, no amount of time that could break up those jelly beans. I turned off the mixer, dumped the mix into the garbage, and vowed that I would never go that route again.

100 PERCENT WHOLE WHEAT BREAD

Gael Watson

We don't make 100 percent stone-ground whole wheat bread very much. Most people like a slightly lighter bread. We make a twelve-grain bread. We cook the twelve-grain cereal first into a porridge and add it to the mix, turning it into 75 percent whole wheat bread. It's a really nice wheat bread, but not 100 percent.

About twenty-five years ago, a man used to come to the bakery who wanted 100 percent whole wheat bread. He would get angry if I hadn't baked it. That's all he wanted. Most of the time I didn't have it, because it's not a popular bread. He was getting frustrated and upset. So I said, "Just tell me when you're coming and I'll make that bread. No problem; just tell me."

He said, "All right. I'll be back on Thursday for my bread."

Thursday came. Fran Aldercott was working that day, but she was taking a break, so I was in the shop. I saw him walking towards the door. I forgot to make the 100 percent whole wheat bread and I couldn't face him. I didn't have time to get out of there, so I dropped down onto the floor and got under the counter.

He came in. "Ding-ding. Ding-ding." I was under the counter and Fran came along and she saw me there. "SHHHH!!"

She asked the man, "Can I help you?"

He said, "I've come for my 100 percent whole wheat bread."

"Mmmm, I don't think we baked that today."

He left the bakery, livid and furious, and there I was, cowering under the counter.

THE DOUGH KNOWS

Gael Watson

I've noticed through all the years that you can tell if the person making the bread is unhappy, or is in a bad mood, or they've been crying. You can tell because the bread reflects it so easily. You can be making bread, and somebody comes in to help you, and they're unhappy. You have made this bread up, it's risen, it's doubled in size, and you've turned it out onto the board. You're cutting it up, and passing it over to this person. The minute they touch it, it affects the bread. Immediately, instantaneously, the bread is affected by the mood of the person who's making it, and it's not going to turn out. It's not going to rise as well as it should, it's not going to have the smell that you need it to have. There have been batches of bread I've thrown out because there's no way you can pass that on to a customer. Not because it doesn't have good ingredients, but because there's sadness in it.

And the reverse is true. Somebody who's elated, happy, looking forward to something, enjoying where they are, and at peace with themselves—they're the ones who make good bread. You can see it. The bread reacts to that—it rises well; it smells good; it tastes delicious. It's wonderful. When you think about it, you're activating yeast, which is a living thing; a living substance. That very simple organism, the yeast, is extremely sensitive to touch and feeling and emotion. As soon as you touch it, it reacts. I've always marveled at it and thought, "This is an amazing thing, working with something so sensitive."

Fresh loaves of bread displayed in the LaHave Bakery shop, c. 1986. (UNKNOWN)

A LAHAVE BAKERY TRADITION

Gael Watson

In the early years, when I was baking a lot, I was always making up new recipes. I wanted to make it more interesting; that's why there are so many different breads. All baking is a matter of taste. The bread that I make is what I like, and

I hope that other people will like it, too. Once, when I called my bread "traditional," someone said, "This isn't "traditional." My only answer to that person was, "It's traditional to me." This is my tradition and almost forty years later, it's become a tradition for all the little babies who started eating the bread and grew up with it.

I would say my bread-making style is very down-to-earth. Some of our breads are only made with unbleached white flour because, if you like eating white bread, that's what you're going to buy. So I was going to make white bread, but I was going to make it better! With milk and honey and eggs. I want bread that has a lot of ingredients in it, so that even if you're just eating bread, you're being nourished.

Our loaves are denser than commercial bread. Not heavier, but denser. When you bite into a slice of our bread, your teeth are cutting it, not pulling and tearing. You have to chew it. I like that. To be able to digest bread well, you have to chew it. In old cookbooks you always see "eat toast." Toast, it's drier. It takes more chewing, so the enzymes in your saliva are really mixing with it, and that makes it easier to digest. Our bread, I mean *all* bread is nicer toasted, but our bread is really good toasted. And even though it's true that fresh bread right out of the oven is harder to digest, it's also delicious. Very satisfying.

Something I love to do is take a loaf of bread that's maybe two days old and put it in the oven for twenty minutes to half an hour. Get it so it's heated right through and the crust is crispy. Then bring it out of the oven, slice it with a good knife, and slather it with butter. Is there anything better?

CHAPTER 8

More Than Bread

COOKING WITH A CONSCIENCE

Peggy Greer

FROM THE VERY BEGINNING, IT WAS IMPORTANT TO GAEL, BEING PART OF THE BACK-to-the-land movement, that her food was nutritious. Real food. She wanted it to have substance. This has been a large part of her success. She never let go of that. People keep coming because it's delicious, nutritious, real food.

Gael Watson

I've made every effort to make the bread, take-home meals, and our other food as clean as I can. In order to do that, I want to know where every food ingredient is coming from, who is growing it, what their philosophy is, how they treat the land, how they treat their animals. In turn, I can have a clear conscience about what I'm making and what I'm offering to people.

Eating with a conscience is just an extension of living with a conscience. You can carry on doing something, eating something, living in a certain way for a long time until some new piece of information becomes available. If that information makes sense to you, then you question what you've been doing, or what you've been eating. That's conscience. You stop, think about it, change your ways. You always have to be flexible and willing to think. Making food and learning about what goes into food and learning about farming practices is really important, because your conscience is a barometer. You don't have to know everything about something, but you need to be able to trust what you're eating.

The end goal is to be able to come up with a way to do the right thing by people—to be honest, to make an effort, to be able to sell so nobody's losing out. It's a goal I think we can achieve. We source ingredients in the best way we can; we can make good food and make it affordable. I don't call the bread or the food that we make "organic," but in almost every case, I'm able to choose better ingredients.

I want the bread to be available to everyone. From the very beginning we had three different prices for it. It is sold at full price the first day. The second day, it is reduced in price quite a bit. On the third day, it goes straight into the freezer, where it's sold very inexpensively. That way I'm able to feel that just about anybody can afford to eat our bread. If there's an overflow, which happens quite a bit in winter, then that bread goes to the food bank. I'm very happy that I can do that. It is very important that as many people as possible are able to eat our bread if they want to.

Bev Kaulback

Through the time I've been there, Gael's gotten more diverse with everything. They're all good products; all homemade in a commercial environment. There are no preservatives; it's all wholesome and healthy food. Mind you, there's a lot of work that goes into it. It goes through many hands, making every product. It's a big process from one end to the other. When you walk in the building, it's nice to see the freezers with the glass doors filled with all the products.

"We did that!" It's something to be proud of.

Laura Pitts

I say it every time I'm downstairs stripping chicken: "At LaHave Bakery, we do everything the hard way." As a vegetarian, I'm cooking chickens—whole chickens—and then stripping the skin off and taking the meat off the bone. We have to do it the long, hard way so that it's ethical and good.

Andra White

Her food is so good! I love her philosophy about food. Wholesome, very heathy, very nutritious food with whole ingredients.

LOCALLY SOURCED

Gael Watson

The other thing we've always done at the bakery is to source local ingredients as much as possible. Where has it been grown? Do I know the person who's producing it? Where is it coming from; what part of the world? How long has it taken to get to the bakery?

It takes a lot of people to make food security work. It's certainly achievable if the various parts of the food chain keep going in a local way. That's why it's really important to encourage people, if they're going to do some food production, to share what they're doing with the people who live in the area. We try to keep our ears to the ground to hear of anybody who's producing something that they would like to sell.

The Wolters are a farm family living in Conquerall Mills, Nova Scotia. The entire family, just about, is involved in producing greens. Herbs and spinach and kale and mesclun. It's a big cheer when the first bags of these wonderful organic greens start coming in. They supply us for almost the entire year. They also have garlic and celery and sometimes carrots. Whatever they're growing they'll bring in, and we offer it for sale.

They are extremely hard workers, and the wonderful thing about the Wolters is they merchandise their greens. They put them right into the fridge. It's either Wanda or Maria who comes with the box of greens, and they'll take out whatever is left that they brought two days ago. Then they replenish and give me a credit. They look after their own thing, and all I have to do is pay them. Sometimes I'll call them three hours after they've been here to tell them it's all gone, but usually they just come every other day. The Wolters's greens are always very popular, really wonderful greens.

We have other people who bring food for us to sell. We've asked them to do their own merchandising, just like the Wolters. It works well for them because they're not waiting for me to call. They look after it, so it's always available. It works for me, too; it's a great system: the Wolters's greens and Elmridge Farm's root vegetables; blueberries—Kate Naugler's father's blueberries, and other local growers' blueberries in season, as well as from Oxford Foods in Oxford, Nova Scotia. It's nice to have a connection to as many people as possible who are bringing food in.

Every year there's something that somebody brings along, and we will add that to the local food that we sell. In the summer, there's even more opportunity to get local produce. We try to offer whatever is growing. Now, because we have two glass-faced fridges and four glass-faced freezers downstairs, we've got a lot of display area. People can see what we've got.

Todd Zinck, the milkman with Farmers Dairy, has supplied the bakery for over twenty years. He comes in with his own key and does the merchandising himself, which is great. I might leave a note: "I need more of this" or "Can you find that?" Sometimes I'll see him, but usually it's phone conversations.

There is a dairy farm near Merigomish, Nova Scotia—Knoydart Farm. It's owned by Angela, Adam, and Frazer Hunter. They produce organic fluid milk. I haven't had milk as good as that in a long time. We are selling it at the bakery. That's a really important addition for us. They also make cheeses—cheddar cheeses—which we sell.

Most of our eggs are free-range eggs and come from Rocky Top Farm in New Ross, Nova Scotia. They bring the eggs to us once a week. The chicken we get comes from Eden Valley Poultry in Berwick, Nova Scotia.

Most of our meat comes from Martock Glen Farm, near Windsor, Nova Scotia, owned by the Oulton family. It's really nice meat. It tastes good; it's clean. The man who delivers it is a really sweet person. I've gradually bought more and more from them.

The scallops come off the scallop dragger just next door—LaHave Seafoods. Ryan Himmelman, you see him coming over with this 50-pound sack on his shoulder every time the boat comes in. So that's kind of a nice thing. Then there's Wayne Crowell from Pubnico, Nova Scotia, who brings in fresh haddock. Also, a man named Wallace brings haddock to us from Digby, Nova Scotia. We sell some of the scallops and haddock fresh the day they come in, and vacuum pack the rest for the freezer. So we have fresh seafood, and fresh-frozen seafood. We are also able to pick up Afishionado sustainable salmon and Arctic char in Bedford, Nova Scotia.

Sadie Watson

The scallops and fish coming in off the boats—Gael has always been like that. A focal point of this business is trying to source everything within one hundred, two hundred kilometres.

Gael Watson

All the honey that we use now comes from Kevin Spicer, who lives in the Annapolis Valley, Nova Scotia. That's a nice relationship, over probably ten, twelve years now—a great boon to have that source of mostly wildflower honey, all from Lunenburg County. It's a lot, almost twelve hundred pounds, just over half a ton a year. Incredible! Think of the bees!

We've been getting our wheat grain from Longspell Point Farm in Kingsport, Nova Scotia, for many years now. The farm is run by Jeff McMahon and family. I admire that family hugely and the farm is beautiful.

The oil that we've been able to get for several years now is cold-pressed canola oil, made from organic canola grown in Heatherdale, Prince Edward Island. The company is called Alpha Mills. It's really beautiful stuff. We also use that same oil in our vinaigrettes and salad dressings. Anything we make that has oil in it, it's always this organic cold-pressed canola.

Sadie Watson

My time away from here has made me realize how unique an opportunity it is to have those very personal connections with producers. Gael's been doing that since 1984 without a break—not only for the last five or ten years since it's re-emerged as a popular and important thing to do. The business has never closed. It has remained open for all that time, for all those producers, and there's been that really important symbiotic connection. It's been a wonderful, amazing, unique thing.

THE LUNCH COUNTER
Gael Watson

Years ago, when we first started the lunch counter, we would get Black Forest ham for the sandwiches. But then I thought, "No, we're going to get the meat and roast it ourselves." We started getting home-smoked, centre-cut hams from Greek's Quality Meats in Bridgewater, Nova Scotia, baking and slicing them ourselves—it's just a nicer sandwich, made with meat that you've cooked. Because, again, when you look into it, meats that are made for sandwiches have additives. And water pumped into them. So we started buying the hams and baking them, and buying the beef, roasting it, and roasting chickens. We really have got into the swing of starting from scratch. To make a sandwich, it's fresh in every way. The bread is fresh. We use mayonnaise, real mayonnaise. We make our own aioli, which is a really nice alternative to ketchup. We use the Wolters's mesclun mix in the sandwiches, as well.

In the beginning, we made filtered coffee in an urn. The lunch counter was busy, and I thought making coffees with an espresso machine would be too time-consuming. I resisted it for years, getting one of those machines. It wasn't until Jesse and Sadie and I went to New Zealand and there was no filtered coffee. It was all espresso. After a month, I was never going back to filtered coffee. So we got an espresso machine for the bakery, and that brought a new wave of making specialty coffees. It was a good thing. A great machine; a good investment.

Andra White

The lunch counter has become more sophisticated over the years. The menu and the special coffees. I just love the food—how it's evolved.

THE SKY'S THE LIMIT

Gael Watson

Sometimes, I lay in bed at night and think, "I wonder...why don't we try making this?" Then I'll do a google search to see what's in it, and what the chances are we can get those ingredients. I'm not looking to complicate anything. It's really simple. When you look at an ingredient list of anything that we sell at the bakery, you know everything that's in it. There's no mystery to it.

I have started producing things that are commonly used. Lately, we have been making ketchup. The tomato is cooked down to be thick, with seasonings in it. The difference with the ketchup that we're making is that there is less sugar in it. We're also making cream of wheat—our own brand of cream of wheat.

We bring in all these wonderful cheeses, and what goes with that is we're making our own crackers. Crackers with butter and they're really tasty. I have a package on my desk all the time.

For quite a few years we've made our own mustards. We make five or six different kinds. We make salad dressings, using the wonderful organic canola oil that comes from Prince Edward Island. Everything is made from scratch. We also make hot sauces. We get cases of Scotch bonnet or jalapeno peppers, depending on what kind of hot sauce we are making.

And, oh my goodness, we started making our own chai because we found commercial chai syrup to be too sweet. On the days we are making chai syrup, it's on the stove all day long, simmering away. The whole place smells of chai. I mean, that's the fun of it. The sky's the limit.

Sadie Watson

Jean Johnston from East LaHave, Nova Scotia, had been doing the jams and chutneys forever, coming in with boxes of them. I said, "Oh my gosh, Jean, we can't possibly sell all that chutney," and it was gone in the first two weeks of the summer. And the marmalade. All the boxes of Seville oranges that come in. Laura has been such a huge part of that, making Grandfather's recipe in the big cauldrons, stirring the marmalade for hours. It always amazes me how much food goes through the shop.

Bev Kaulback

The lady who supplied our jam was retiring. Gael asked me, "How do you feel about making jam?"

"Well, I can try." So, over the years now, I do all kinds of jams and chutneys. The curried apple chutney—absolutely wonderful-tasting chutney. I do a strawberry jam and I do a mango–jalapeno pepper jelly. I do relishes.

I started at the bakery baking bread. I still bake bread, and now I make so many other things. I do muffins and scones. We do savoury and sweet scones. And spinach wraps; they're only made for the bakery, for our breakfast wraps. They're the size of a dinner plate. It's labour-intensive, but when you're in the zone and doing them, it's very therapeutic.

BUTTER

Gael Watson

I was asked, "What do you use for pastry?" I couldn't use lard because too many people didn't eat animals or animal fat. I learned that the most flaky pastries are made with hard fats that have a high melting point. So I used shortening; the most expensive shortening. The problem was, I couldn't get the stuff off my hands. I had to use Gojo industrial cleaner. One day, I was softening the shortening in the microwave and I forgot about it. It melted out—poured out of the microwave—and it was just a mess all over the table. I had to get the Gojo again—to clean up something that we eat. And I thought, "Forget about the lard; forget about the shortening. I'm going to use butter," because butter is better and I can wash it off with hot water; don't even need soap.

"Let's use butter in pastry." Outrageously expensive! Despite all my efforts, I could never get the Dairy Commission to sell me butter at a price that was affordable. Eventually, I had to give up on them. Everyone was pointing out to me that the big grocery stores put butter on cheap every once in a while, so that's what I've been doing; I buy butter on sale. We use it in all the sweets and for the pastry. We use close to five thousand pounds of butter a year. It was a big move to make pies with all-butter crusts—and they are wonderful pies.

TAKE-HOME DINNERS

Gael Watson

We dabbled with the idea of take-home dinners, but it didn't start in earnest until about ten years ago, when I got a second-hand vacuum-pack machine. I realized that machine was really going to change things up. We could make things and freeze them, and they would stay in really good condition.

Bev Kaulback

We vacuum pack all our take-home dinners. Meat pies, chicken pies, scallop pies, mac and cheese, shepherd's pie, and lentil shepherd's pie. Between all of us, we vacuum pack the food, label it, and make sure it's good to go in the freezers. Fruit pies and fresh seafood, too; it goes on and on. It's amazing how much food we do.

Gael Watson

We're making all kinds of meat pies. The beef pies are all made from roasts that we get from Oulton's. We roast chicken that we get from Eden Valley and make that meat into pies, too. Lately, we've been making beef stew with Oulton's beef. It's made with these wonderful golden beets from Longspell Point Farm, where we get the wheat—and parsnips, as well.

We are using expensive ingredients, and it takes a long time to make these meat pies. It's about a three-day process. It's several stages to the end product. It's really the Industrial Revolution all over again, the people involved. It's all made by people doing all these different things.

We make scallop pies. The tourtière is ground pork and beef mixed together, and it's a bit spicy with cloves. That's a really nice one. Lately, we've been making baked beans, which took quite a few tries to get what I thought was a good baked bean recipe—not too sweet, not too much molasses. It's made with chopped tomatoes as well, and bacon. I love them. We also do a vegetarian version.

A Fair Banks Grocery cooler for take-home dinners, butter-crust pies, and local meat and fish, c. 2020. (JANE MORRIGAN)

MORE THAN BREAD

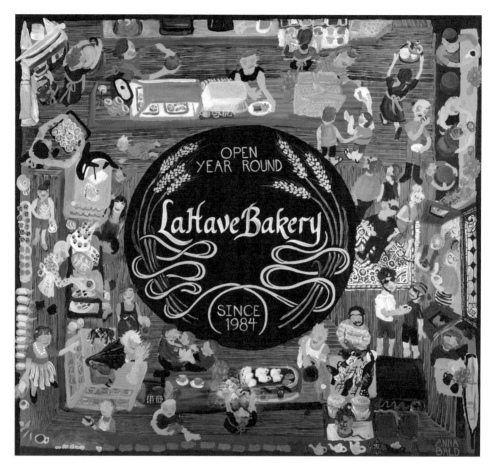

Anna Bald's 2016 painting, LaHave Bakery Since 1984, *features employees and customers from that time. It still hangs in the building.* (Artwork Anna Bald, photo Jim Bell)

We just keep adding new meals. If somebody has an idea, it's "Let's try it." If, after a while, it's not popular, we stop making it. That's the freedom of having a small business. You can try it, and if it doesn't work out, then you can stop doing it.

One young woman, Rielle Doucet, made a really nice recipe she called a vegan stew. It's a combination of all different vegetables that she has roasted first. It's completely interesting and delicious. That won a prize in my head. That was a good one.

Then there's the Haddock au Gratin. It's fresh haddock with a cheesy sauce poured over it, and a butter and toasted-bread topping, with a little parmesan added. That's a Susan Ivany contribution to our repertoire. We make that on a day when the haddock comes in fresh. We've taken that idea and do a Chicken au Gratin as well, exactly in the same way.

CHAPTER 9

More Than a Bakery

A GIGANTIC BUILDING

Gael Watson

THE BUILDING IS SITTING ONE-THIRD OVER THE WATER. IT WAS BUILT WITH PIERS underneath it. It's 110 feet long and 60 feet across, with three storeys in the front and three storeys in the back. When you come in the front door from the road, you're coming into the original LaHave Outfitting Company shop, with the tin ceilings and the cabinets and the shelves. It's got the biggest radiator I've ever seen sitting in the middle of the room—the only heat for the shop.

When we first got the LaHave Outfitters, my main focus was the bakery and renovating the building. As it got renovated and more spaces became safe to use, more things could happen in it.

MARINE SERVICES

Gael Watson

Early on, we had this little marina. We encouraged people to use the wharf and, not that long after, Mike also built floating docks in deeper water so that people could come in. We bought a boat, the *Seal*, a North Sea trawler yacht.

It was this cheery little 30-foot boat built by Stewart MacKay. We had a lot of fun on that boat. Mike had a little business taking people out to the LaHave Islands. We had marine services, such as refilling divers' scuba tanks, moorings, fresh water, electrical plug-ins, a shower, washrooms, laundromat, and food. I also made bread mixes for boaters so they could make fresh bread at sea. Quite a few people took me up on it. It wasn't really a bustling business, but it was certainly used.

The North Sea trawler yacht, the Seal, *built by Stright-Mackay, Ltd. in Pictou, NS. It was used by Mike Watson to take people on tours of the LaHave Islands and area, c. 1990.* (UNKNOWN)

Sadie Watson

The marine aspect of the property was huge. There were people in little boats from all over the place. I was always interfacing with the rest of the world; it was a real hub in that way. People often describe the bakery as the community hub, but growing up I felt like it was a touchstone for people from all over the world as well, which definitely influenced and inspired me. I loved it here, but clearly I was going to leave at a certain point. Part of that was because I was meeting all of these people, hearing all these languages. I spent my whole childhood on the water, so I was very connected to living coastal. I think being connected to the water and the ocean has really been grounding and calming for me.

Peggy Greer

Gael has maintained all that, the nautical aspect. You see all kinds of boats come there. When you come down the hill and around the corner, you often see yachts off the bakery, and smaller boats alongside the wharf and slipway. It's just amazing—coastal cruisers who come from all along the eastern seaboard. An open boat of young people from a boat school in Halifax takes refuge at the bakery as they're going along the coast. And the kids from the LaHave Yacht Club, summer sailing lessons, have their big final day sailing to the bakery and having lunch. Even the shark research ship takes cover off the wharf, and the crew go to the bakery. Of course!

INTERNATIONAL HOSTEL

Gael Watson

On the top floor of the building is a large, old apartment. From 1917 to 1922, the Canadian Bank of Commerce was there. You had to go all the way up the stairs to the bank. But then the brick building across the road was built and the bank moved there. Eventually that building was sold to the Royal Bank. For the first year or so after we bought the building, the apartment was rented out. In the summer of '86, we moved into it as a family, after Mike came back from sea. Because it was big, we also used it as an international hostel for twenty years. We met a lot of really interesting people during that time.

The hostel was very popular for quite a long time—fifteen years at least. That was in the days when people were travellers. It wasn't really tourism; it was people wanting to get to know the community they were passing through. They might stay, and they might help in the bakery, and we'd get to know them—people, a couple, or one person on a bicycle. You just never see that

The LaHave Bakery's third-storey apartment, c. 2020; the space was used for twenty years as an International Youth Hostel and a Marine Hostel. (JANE MORRIGAN)

anymore. When did it begin that people started getting scared? That's when it stopped. People didn't feel safe travelling on their own or hitchhiking. That's out, especially now. But for a long time, it was so acceptable to be backpacking across country. Australians who would come over, they weren't going to come this distance and spend a night. They were in Canada for a year or two. Because of that, we got to know them and corresponded with them. It was really fun sharing that place with strangers.

People would come in out of the cold. One time, this young man came to the door. It was dark; a freezing cold night. Knock, knock. He was soaked to the bone. Shivering. I had made spaghetti; it smelled wonderful.

"Come in." I poured a bath for him. He went into the bath, stayed there until he was warm, and came out in dry clothes. "Come in and join us at the table."

"What are you having?"

"Spaghetti."

"What's the meat?"

I said, "It's pork." He was so hungry. He was Jewish, and you could see it on his face, that struggle between hunger and faith. In the end, he decided not to join us for spaghetti. I made him something else. That stays with me.

People on boats would come in and stay a little while. One day, standing on the wharf, Kevin Wambach, who'd taken over the boat shop, had his binoculars out. He said, "You see that tiny little boat out there?"

I said, "Yeah," and he said, "Well, there's a British flag flying on the stern." The man on that boat was named Frank Dye. He was a machinist in his sixties from Norfolk, England, I think. He was travelling all over the place, in a Wayfarer dinghy with a sail—a single sail. He stayed that winter at the hostel. A really intrepid older man.

Sadie Watson

There are so many aspects to the experience of this place. Cyclists and hitchhikers and that type of travel just isn't happening in the same way here now. The buses are largely gone; there are no trains. It's less and less accessible to people who don't have a car, or who don't have wealth to travel. But back then, there were lots of young women who were backpacking, and young men. German travelers, Austrian, Australian, Singaporean, Italian, French. I remember this Japanese couple who came through. For a long time the hostel was fully booked. I got to sit at the big table and hang out with all these people, and they would share their food and their stories. Most of them seemed old to me, but they were probably just late teens, or in their twenties and thirties.

Gael Watson

The highest we ever charged was twelve dollars per person. I think it started at six or seven dollars. The idea was to make it affordable, so that people who didn't have a lot of money could travel and be in safe, warm places overnight. And there used to be quite a few hostels. There was one in Liverpool, New Ross, and Halifax. It was quite a thing. Then, more and more groups of people wanted to stay, and we didn't have the room. We only had beds for seven people. The thing that actually made us turn the corner and say no was that, in order to get our license, we needed to have bars on the windows. I just couldn't go for it. Not doing bars on the windows; I'm not going that far.

BIRD ROOM

Gael Watson

There's a room at the very end of the second floor, overlooking the river, that we call the "bird room." The bird room initially began in 1986, after we moved into the apartment. It was very rough, like a barn. That's where I kept my hens from our place. It was a chicken coop for years. After we moved back to the house, we made the room into a really nice office. That's where the bookkeeping for the bakery happened. When my mother died, I inherited some of her finches, budgies, and lovebirds. I put them in the office. They started off in cages, but then I got a couple of parrots, small parrots, who soon started entertaining themselves by opening up cage doors. The birds flying around—and their droppings—made the room harder to use as an office. One day, one of the parrots chewed into the computer line. She got a shock. It didn't kill her, but once birds know the freedom of flight, you can't take that away. The office was moved. Now, parrots and canaries, budgies, and finches live in that room. Most of them fly free. The bird room is the best room in the whole building. Beautiful, but it's been chewed around the edges a bit.

Andra White

When I started bookkeeping for the bakery, I had the bird room. I had my own room back there. I loved that, and I loved the birds. Jesse would come in and say, "How can you stand the sound of those birds?" But I loved it. When you come in, they start squawking a lot, but then they go quiet after a little bit. When one of the parrots almost got electrocuted, we had to shift my office into Gael's office.

LAHAVE CRAFT CO-OP

Gael Watson

When you come into the building from the side door and enter the alleyway, the LaHave Craft Co-op is on your right. The original cornerstone of the co-op was an outrageous, brilliant, and talented man—Robert Wikstrom, better known as "Wick."

That first year, the first people were Wick, Kathryn Gordon, Odette Van Tassel, Kathy Fisher, and Barb Smith. It has been operating since 1993. There are more than thirty local craftspeople who sell their wares there, all of it made locally and by hand to this day. After Wick died, Marnie Troyer and Kathryn Gordon headed it up. Several of the original members are still with the co-op.

The craft co-op is in the space where the fish plant used to be a hundred years ago. The room has a very warpled floor. You can see by the floor the years of trundling barrels full of salt. That floor was the main fish-curing and packing area, before they started freezing the fish. Right up until 1935 the fish was cured and sent to the Caribbean. There used to be very few windows, so it was quite a dark place to work. I think that on each level there were four very small windows that were spaced out. Very little has been done in that room, other than the wall is new; the south wall with all the big windows, with its huge beams and wooden floor. The co-op comes in early in the spring, and each person sets up their tables.

Kathryn Gordon

A group of us opened up a craft co-operative. It started off with about eight local craftspeople and artists and has grown to over thirty. Every member of the co-op feels personally attached to the craft store, I think. One of the reasons it is such a unique store is that we are all responsible for our own spaces—displaying, replenishing, keeping it clean. There are so many different styles throughout the shop. We all have a vote in all matters, and majority wins. There is no hierarchy, and we all take turns shopkeeping. One member is the bookkeeper. Approximately 80 percent of our members are women. In the early days, we were between 90 and 95 percent women, but that has changed somewhat.

HOMEGROWN SKATEBOARDS

Gael Watson

The third floor, the top floor, is where you'll find Homegrown Skateboards. Jesse Watson has been running that for twenty-five years. He makes skateboards and he silkscreens. He also has a huge bowl for skating.

The LaHave Craft Co-op, c. 2015. Co-op member Fran Aldercott stands at the cash.
(JANE MORRIGAN)

Jesse was into skateboarding when he was young. When he was seventeen, he built his own press. He started off on the bottom floor, back in the area we called "the dungeon," where the freezers and staff room are now. From there, he moved up to the top floor because nothing was really going on in that back section. Also, where the building had been cut off, where it had collapsed, there was a part that was higher than the rest. Since the roof was gone off that section, we decided to bump it up for better views. It turned out it was the perfect space for Jesse to, first of all, have his ramp, and then, later, the bowl. It's an amazing thing to have on the top of a very old building overlooking the LaHave River. The structure is different, but the bump is what Jesse took advantage of for skateboarding.

It's a huge space. On one side is where the silkscreening happens and where he makes the boards, so that's the industry part. On the other side is his retail shop and a stage. Then there's the bowl, which looks like a swimming pool only it has no water in it. Jesse's used the space for all sorts of events and fixed it up beautifully. It's really nice, the way he has it.

Jesse Watson

I was excited about trying to make skateboards. From all those skateboarding magazines, I could tell that the art was a big part of it. I'd always doodled and drawn, so I knew that would carry over into graphics. Also, I learned the fundamentals of silkscreening in art class in high school. I started full-on, spending nights working on the first press. Researching more and more, whatever I could find. Talking to boatbuilders, talking to cabinetmakers, and learning about tools more.

All these things started to combine, really taking traction. Down on the bottom floor, exactly where the staff room is now, I stapled blankets up because it was super-drafty and freezing cold. I would layer up with gloves. I started building the different divisions: a paint room; the pressing room, with vapour-barrier hallways. The press was the centre of it all. The first batches, over the first couple of years, all came out of there. So I was making the boards downstairs and was skateboarding on the top floor. I think it was '98 or '99 that I started gradually moving everything to the top floor. Not having a time limit on it was the biggest asset in getting that space fixed up. That was huge.

It's the never-ending excitement of making things. Every single batch, I get this crazy nervous rush, because I can't 100 percent know what's going to happen. And then to be able to make a skateboard from scratch and skate it, finished, in the same space—like cradle to the grave—that's key to tapping into something.

PUBLISHER'S OFFICE

Gael Watson

Early on, Michael Atkins, a publisher from Ontario, asked if we could build an office for him. There was space on the second floor. I was thinking fairly small—ten by twelve or something. Jesse's opinion was when you have a building that size, you shouldn't have little rooms. And I have gone with that at every turn. It makes so much sense. If you have a big building, why put small rooms in it? It just feels good to have larger spaces. The office is about twenty-six by sixteen. We made it quite nice, with spruce floors. One big room overlooking the river, with a little propane fireplace and a long wooden boardroom table. It's a lovely room. Michael rented the office for over twenty years.

THE GALLERY
Gael Watson

To the right of the publisher's office on the second floor is a room I usually call "the weaving room." Lately, it's known as "the gallery." It was a large room, in rough shape, that was used for weaving workshops beginning in 2000. Leslie Armstrong, who used to teach at the Nova Scotia College of Art and Design, asked if she could use the room to teach people how to weave. I told her my mother was a weaver and said, "I would love for that to happen." There must have been at least eight floor looms. From my office, I could hear the thump-thumping of the looms.

The weaving workshops eventually came to an end in LaHave. It was sad to see them go. When they left, I conferred with Jesse about how far we would go to fix that room up. In the end, we decided to keep the room the size that it is, which is huge, and finish it out. Finish the windows, put frames around the windows. The floors were in terrible shape. Ross Morrison and his friend Michael Higgins pulled all the old floorboards up. Fortunately, there were two layers, so there was enough wood to choose from—just enough—to re-cover the entire floor. Homegrown Skateboards was above that room, so we put in a ceiling with more insulation. Then it became a gallery space, used in the summertime for people to display and sell their artwork.

Peggy Greer

There have been many shows there with lots of artists—many who would not have a chance to show their work anywhere else. They can have an opening with friends and family and feel a real sense of comfort. Gael has created a beautiful space with lovely light coming in those big windows. Her openness to all sorts of creative souls allows that gallery to be busy.

GAEL'S OFFICE

Gael Watson

For many years, my office was right next to the shop. The time came, in 2012, when we needed more space to prepare lunches. It was hard to leave my office downstairs because it was so connected to the shop. Looking at the way the building was configured, I realized that we could put an office on the second floor and it could actually overlook the shop. When the new office was built, we made three small windows in the wall so that we could look down into the shop below. Just like the old Woolworth's stores. When things get really busy, especially in the summer, we can see what's happening, so we can jump up and go down and help. Even though it's on the second floor, the office is still attached to the shop. There's so much happening in the building these days, so it's a very busy office.

The other reason I didn't want to leave my old office is because of the safe. It's a really useful thing, but no easy task getting it up the stairs. When I realized that the safe could be moved, I was ready to make the leap. That happened one day when I was watching the crane on the delivery truck unloading sheets of plywood and lumber for the new office upstairs. I went outside; I was standing beside the driver as he manipulated the wood and asked him how heavy a load could he lift with that crane. He was quite confident of what he could do with it. I said, "Well, I bet you couldn't lift a thousand-pound safe," and he said, "Oh yeah. Yeah, I could do that."

When he was finished unloading the lumber, I showed him the safe. "You could move this and lift it up through the window on the second floor?" He said, "Sure. Piece of cake." A bunch of people got together and, with great effort, moved the safe out onto my little porch. Then we took out the window on the second floor which, fortunately, is a big window. Just inside that window we had attached a block and tackle to a ceiling beam. The man lifted the safe up with the crane, and we hooked the chain to it. This huge safe was swung, very carefully, through the opening, and down onto the second floor. From there, again with a lot of effort, it was moved into the new office. That's where it sits, and probably will—hopefully—forever!

LAHAVE RIVER BOOKS

Gael Watson

LaHave River Books opened on July 13, 2016. The space was formerly a boat shop, set up to finish a schooner built by Covey Island Boatworks called the *Tree of Life*. Kevin Wambach, a fine carpenter and cabinetmaker, moved in after that, and he rented it for his own boat shop, right up until 2015. It was one of the parts of the building that was still pretty rough. So when Kevin left, I felt I needed to turn it into something really special.

Andra White

One day in 2015 Gael and I were talking upstairs in the office. Gael said, "I was thinking about opening a bookstore. What do you think?"

I was like, "Ohhh!" I was just so excited. We both love books and we always talked about books. I said, "That's a great idea; just a wonderful idea." She had thought about partnering up with Ron Topp, who used to own Sagor's Bookstore in Bridgewater. That was such a loss to the community.

Gael said, "I'm going to talk to Ron," and I said, "Yeah, yeah." She got right on the phone and called him. She met with him, over coffee, at the shop. Afterward, Gael came upstairs and said, "Ron said no."

I said, "Oh, that's so disappointing. That was such a great idea."

The LaHave marine woodworking shop was renovated to construct LaHave River Books, c. 2016. Rob Muise was the carpenter. (JANE MORRIGAN)

Then she said, "Well, would you like to open the bookstore with me?"

I said, "What? I have no experience with anything like that. No experience running a business. I have no money. I have nothing."

Gael said, "Well, let's not worry about anything like that. Would you?" And I said, "Yeah! Yeah!" It was like a dream. Gael had such vision. She could exactly say how it was all going to be. She saw it right away.

Gael Watson

When I talked to Andra White, she was keen, so we became partners in LaHave River Books. Andra's the one who runs it, and I was the one to design the room with the bookshelves and the seating. A lot of people call it a library because it has that feeling about it. It's a wonderful room, at the very end of the building, overlooking the water.

It's a very large, open room. Because the building was made to hold tons of salt that came up from the Turks and Caicos, there are very heavy beams to support the upper floors. Almost every single beam has got two big wooden knees coming off it, one on each side. The floor was very wobbly, so we laid a new floor down, and over that floor there are kilim wool rugs and some Persian rugs. Built into the walls are bookshelves, and the bookshelves are arranged so that one section is free books, another section is gently used books, and another section is new books for sale. Rob Muise, the carpenter, and I worked with cardboard boxes until we got the most comfortable arrangement for a horseshoe-shaped bookcase for the new books. There's a raised cement platform from the old days, which we covered with a wooden floor. That's where we put an old library table that came from Trinity College, University of Toronto. It's about nine feet long by four feet wide, and was built in the early 1800s. This magnificent table, with its one-inch-thick wooden top, is a feature of that room. There are lots of plants in the windows, and rattan furniture to sit and read if you care to. When the two big wooden doors are open, you can look straight out onto the wharf and the water. In the summer, with those doors open, the fresh air coming in, and the sun reflecting on the water, it's really pretty special.

Andra White

Gael always had her free library upstairs in the lunchroom of the bakery. So she said, "We'll bring that downstairs." People heard that they could bring their used books here. We sort through them, and a lot of them are in really good shape. Gael came up with the idea of five-dollar and ten-dollar books. That turned out to be such a good thing, because it gives the bookstore the extra money it needs to keep going.

On opening day, we had so much support from the community. That was a great day, and we did really well. In the beginning, there would be days where nobody came in, but Gael's philosophy with the bakery has always been, "Be available. Be open seven days a week." So we do the same thing, just not through the winter anymore because it's so expensive to heat the space. With our online web store, we do really well in the winter now. And, because of Covid, it's normal for people to shop that way.

Gael Watson

I thought the bookstore needed an old piano. I remembered that Paul Newton, a physician at the hospital who has been coming to the bakery for years, had said several years before that he had an old piano to give away. I called him and asked, "Do you still have that old piano?" He said, "Yes, but it's up to you to come and get it." So the next weekend we went and got it and installed it in the bookstore. It's an upright grand, probably a hundred years old. It has a little sign on it that says, "Feel Free to Play Me." There are so many people who can play the piano, and will sit down and play. The room is perfect for it.

Andra White

I've met so many amazing people here, so that's been really great. I've learned more about books, so many books, and so many new writers. I've met some great writers. I remember Michael Ondaatje came in. That was the most amazing thing for me. I was too shy to talk to him. But Michael Ondaatje came in to our bookstore. And it was, "Holy cow!"

There's something for everyone here. If you don't have money, you can get free books. Even if you have money, you can get free books. Some people like to find a gem in the free books. There are other people who like a fresh, brand-new book. We started having readings. At first, there were a few readings a year, and then it became every Thursday night. It was really popular. A lot of local writers launched their books here, which added another level to the bookstore. April is poetry month, when we showcase poetry. A few concerts here too, because all the wood is great for absorbing sound. Every year, sales get a little better. We get more and more support all the time.

Peggy Greer

They have readings of new novels, poetry, and non-fiction. Again, such a welcoming, warm, and comfortable space makes it possible to share with friends and neighbours. To feel the love, really, the love of the artists and writers—the love of the whole community. Gael has created safe spaces, sacred spaces.

Outdoor waterfront seating at the LaHave Bakery and LaHave River Books, c. 2021. (JANE MORRIGAN)

CHAPTER 10

Fair Banks Grocery

THE TOY GROCERY STORE

Gael Watson

I'VE ALWAYS WANTED A GROCERY STORE. WHEN I WAS EIGHT YEARS OLD, MY FAVOU-rite toy was a cardboard-brick grocery store. It was a Christmas present out of the Eaton's catalogue. I would play with it for hours. I remember carting it up to the top of our street and selling lemonade out of it—spring, summer, and fall. I loved that cardboard grocery store. These things that appeal to us stay with us. So I never gave up on that idea. One day, the time will be right!

THE REAL GROCERY STORE

Gael Watson

So this lifelong image of a grocery store began to unfold. For one thing, it's a big building; there was room. Secondly, the bakery is already producing food, and we can make more of that food. It's that "value-added" idea of business.

There wasn't enough room in the shop to sell more food. But downstairs there was a space across from the bread-packing area. It used to be a room filled with recyclables and anything that anybody didn't want to see. We called it "the dungeon" because it was so dark and nasty. Jesse had the idea to open up the wall, remove the big plank door, and clean the room up. He carefully cleaned the old Fairbanks Morse engine in there; the pieces of copper and brass gleaming. When he came home from a trip to Europe, I asked him, "What ideas have you got?" He saw a panel of windows all along the wall. So now there's a row of windows in that room, facing Himmelman Supply. Once the windows were in—once the light came in—we thought it would make a great little fishery museum. Then I decided to use part of it for my new mill room.

Sadie and I had visited a new "tare" shop in Halifax, and having one with the same idea in LaHave made good sense. The idea of a tare shop is that you bring your own vessels and containers and fill them, therefore using fewer new materials.

Rob Muise was the one who really put the work into scraping that floor. It was so saturated with oil; the floor was really filthy. He got down on his hands and knees and he scraped it all by hand. Then he sanded it, and there's this beautiful, beautiful floor. I asked him if he would make a replica of the upstairs counters for the grocery store. It's the main focus, and it's magnificent. The rest of it came together; different people participated. We added the walk-in fridge, a battery of chest freezers and upright freezers, to store the food. We decided to name the grocery store "Fair Banks Grocery" after the Fairbanks Morse engine, which had been installed in 1935 to freeze the fish instead of salt-curing the fish; also because being fair is what the bakery strives to do, and the building sits on the banks of the LaHave River.

The Fair Banks Grocery under construction, with the Fairbanks engine cleaned up, c. 2019. The mill room is to the right. (JANE MORRIGAN)

Andra White

The grocery store is just amazing, too! The seed of the idea came before Covid. Laura and I often comment that we feel Gael is part witch because she seems to know what's coming down the line before it even comes down the line. So the grocery store was under way; the renovations were happening.

Over the years, Gael has picked apart all different parts of the building. In the beginning, that space was just full of stuff. But then Jesse and Gael decided to make it kind of a museum, because of that really cool cooling system that was in place. Gael wanted to bring that out and show it, and there were a lot of photographs. People thought it was really neat, but then Gael decided that's where she'd like to have the grocery store.

Gael Watson

We opened Fair Banks Grocery on May 1, 2020, and we've been, ever since, just expanding and expanding. Getting more things that people ask for, hearing through the grapevine about more things that people are making, growing.

The grocery store has got the very same appeal as it did when I was eight and only imagining things. As I've come to realize, imaginings can be quite solid if you start being serious about making an idea a real thing. You soon discover, over time, that all you have to do is put all the pieces together so you can make that idea into a real thing.

IT JUST MAKES SENSE

Gael Watson

It was making more sense. We needed more and more room to sell what we were making. We had moved into making so many different things because of the need for everyone who wanted to work to have a job. It began with "Donald Robertson's Marmalade," my father's recipe. So the marmalade was the germ, the beginning of the idea.

The grocery store is a whole new thing, but it's so connected into what we're already doing. We already have a lot of dry goods because of the bakery.

The bread cooling and packing area at the Lahave Bakery, c. 2018. (JANE MORRIGAN)

There was already that core. The bakery was built to hold food and keep food safe. The kitchens were all built to make food safely. All the equipment I had bought over the years—the vacuum pack sealer, the Hobarts, everything I had—came into more use. It was very industrious. Everybody was being very industrious. It was just a little sort of hop to the next level of doing business.

The beauty of turning it, keeping everything fresh, was that the bakery is always making food. So all our flour is really fresh, and you never have to worry about how old that spice might be, because we're getting it frequently. Fresh. Lots of spice. It's just a wonderful smell when it's fresh, so we have that advantage. As Ruby said, "Oh, we've had our advantages." Well, that was an advantage—that we'd been doing this for years.

Kathryn Gordon

I love it. Gael decided to do it, centred around the engine room. I love the name of the grocery store. And the bakery itself, over the years, has become more of a grocery store anyway. Over the past ten years or so, we've been able to buy milk and some vegetables, frozen meals. It was timed perfectly with the pandemic. Although it was in Gael's mind for a lot longer, the timing couldn't be better. It's just another fabulous facet of the bakery.

A GOING CONCERN

Gael Watson

We didn't start the grocery store because of Covid. We had been planning it for over a year. It was just complete coincidence that when the grocery store was almost ready, Covid came along. The grocery store began under circumstances that we never could have imagined. So the timing was perfect. Had we only been able to sell our lunches and our bread, there's no way that we would be able to support twenty people. So there were twenty people who never needed to lose their jobs. We just kept rolling with the grocery store. I started bringing in more and more essentials, and it became more appealing to people. Within a year of opening, it was a real going concern.

Andra White

The grocery store was already coming, probably for the summer business, but Gael ramped it up a little when Covid hit. And, holy cow, there you go. It saved the bakery that year. Boy, is it ever popular. All those homemade pies! I eat them all the time—the fruit pies and the meat pies. What an amazing thing, and it just keeps evolving and evolving. It's great. You don't really have to go to Bridgewater anymore if you don't want to.

Kathryn Gordon

It's so convenient. It's also supporting small business. Being able to buy Gael's bread and, at the same time, frozen pies, sweets, I think it has great importance. And for tourists and campers to be able to have all their needs met, right in this area, is a real bonus. The LaHave Bakery, the LaHave Outfitters, has become a destination for people.

Peggy Greer

Yeah, the grocery shop. The timing of that. Let's face it, Gael's brilliant at timing. It was great that she could create such a beautiful space and, once again, give back to the community. When Covid came, no one had to go to big stores. You could get what you wanted online and have it brought to your car, right in the community. And she has continued to source great stuff that has to meet her standards, so you know it's got to be good. Some local people do all their shopping there. One more gift from Gael to the community.

THE FUN OF IT

Gael Watson

It's just fun! I keep saying, "I'm playing grocery." I guess it's because I used to have so much fun with my cardboard grocery store, my favourite toy. Fair Banks Grocery is a fun project for me.

Laura Pitts

The grocery store right now is beyond—it's the funnest. It's way more fun than running a restaurant. I love running a grocery store. Just sitting there and saying, "What do I need to go to Bridgewater for? Let's not go there. Let's see if I can find it; order it in." Massive amounts of ordering. It feels like I'm playing a fun game, and then you talk to the people who are working there; we have a really good group of people. They're saying, "Oh, customers are really loving this," or, "A lot of customers are asking for that." Most fun ever. The grocery store is the greatest thing that ever happened to us.

CHAPTER 11

Covid Times

NAVIGATING COVID

Gael Watson

AT FIRST, WE WERE MEETING PEOPLE AT THE DOOR: "YOU CAN COME THROUGH IF you sanitize your hands." Very shortly after that, we had to close the doors. Then it was, "Call and we'll take your orders." We printed out a list of what we had, with our phone number, and included the list with the orders. People were really not wanting to go into Bridgewater, into the larger stores—just wanting to stay away and stay safe. Because the bakery is in a rural place, away from other businesses, people would just come to the door and pick up their orders. We had a table outside the door. It was a pretty good system. Customers would call or order online. We'd put the order together and tell them how much. They would pay by e-transfer or Visa. If it was cash, which we accepted, it had to be in an envelope—exact change.

When the doors could open again, Covid meant people had to come in, one at a time, six feet apart. It also meant we could speak to them at the door and say, "This is what we're doing. You need to keep your distance. Please sanitize your hands." The person at the door would explain, "Over to your left is where you can order your coffee, teas, and drinks. Keep going and you can order your lunch," and then, "It's a one-way street, so please keep going; keep your distance." It sounds a bit stifling, but in actual fact it personalized the business. We were people talking to people, and they could ask us questions and we could answer them individually.

Right off the bat, when the provinces closed down, we didn't have that intensity of summer. The push of those two months, of having to hire enough people to look after the numbers of customers that come through, was gone. I think a lot of customers don't realize how much pressure there is on people who work behind the counter during the summer. In such large numbers, there's a tension that goes along with having a pulse of people. With Covid restrictions, the stress level came right down, even though it's a serious disease. We took measures and made changes, following what the Department of Health was saying we needed to do. But it was to our benefit, too, that we were making these changes.

LaHave Bakery customers in the shop during Covid, c. 2021. (JANE MORRIGAN)

WEATHERING THE PANDEMIC

Gael Watson

We were putting together the last bits of Fair Banks Grocery when Covid came along—"da-da-DAH!" There was a real need for the grocery store, and it expanded quickly because of Covid. Very quickly, when I think of it. Gosh.

We had to reduce our breakfast and lunch menus. All along, we had been making take-home meals, but it was the pies that caught the attention of more people because they are wonderful pies. People not being able to go out to restaurants, and yet wanting to have a break from making a meal, that's when they really became popular. It was the take-home dinners and the pies that were the stars that helped us through Covid.

Laura Pitts

So we have a shortened menu, just five things that are really good, and everybody's happy with it. Then you go downstairs and buy a loaf of bread, a bag of grapes, some butter, and some milk, and off you go. And you're happy.

Gael Watson

The money that came from the government to help during Covid enabled me to move ahead a lot faster, to keep up with the need. The security of having it there. And it certainly kept us all employed.

Andra White

Covid was a really stressful time. Laura was super-vigilant about how the bakery was going to run. She took charge of that. That was the best thing, I think, at the end of the day, because there was no waffling. If there was any sign of Covid anywhere close by, it would have been shut down. And that's really good. That whole year, it was stressful. I'm sure it was like that for most businesses. But then there's Gael: "How is everybody?" Just getting through it, and going with it, and just being, "Yup—okay. Let's do this. Let's do that." Gael always wants to be hospitable. That's really hard, to have an environment such that customers want to come back and, at the same time, to be hypervigilant. It was different, but you adjust and look on with pure respect that they did all of this.

VERY "OLD WORLD"

Gael Watson

Oddly enough, Covid made serving customers more social and friendly. People looked at you when they asked for something. They had masks and we had masks, so eye contact became really important. It's amazing how much expression there is in the eyes. You actually can tell if somebody is smiling or frowning and there's a lot of body language happening. It's pretty interesting.

When a person would come down the stairs and see the array of freezers, fridges, baskets of things, things on the shelves, we immediately approached them and said, "Let me know if there's anything you'd like. I will get it for you." If a person said, "Yes, I have a number of things," we'd get one of the baskets, a witherod or wicker basket, and we'd collect it for them. "Here's a jug of milk, here is a frozen dinner, here is some meat, and here is some spinach." We'd put it all in the basket, and we'd ring it through.

It's a new way of doing things, but it's also an old way of doing things. The days when the LaHave Outfitters shop was operating—in the 1910s, '20s, '30s, '40s, '50s—all of what they had for sale was behind the counter. People would have to go up to the counter and ask for something. It wasn't a self-serve society, shopping in those days. It was: you asked for something and then you were served. So, in a way, there is a similarity between the old ways and the ways during Covid.

For years, I've said the shop doesn't work well because everything is behind the counters. Well, during Covid, the shop was perfect. You just have to wait long enough for things to change. I think once people get used to this new way of doing things—in fact a very old way—they'll really like it. We don't want to lose that added personal service. You can see that customers just appreciate it, and it gives us an opportunity to explain what's in something, or where it came from, pointing out, "Oh, if you like that, you might be interested in this."

It's very Old World. It's a little bit like theatre, too. The music is on; the reel of the day. The music is playing, the mood is good. Staff are getting their breaks when they need their breaks. It's slowed down so that we notice what needs to be done. If you're moving too fast, you don't even know what isn't working well. Slowing down has been a really good thing.

CALMER WATERS

Gael Watson

Covid coming along has been a real game changer, I think, for just about everybody—because it's not normal. Because nothing of the way we live these days is the same as it was. Covid has changed things around for us, and a lot of it's for the better.

We continue serving people on a one-on-one basis because we think it's a better way, anyway. It's more personal, and we can address what people are looking for. In the summer, I have more people available to serve. People don't mind at all being served, but if they have to wait, they do mind.

The plan is to stay with just two little tables in the lunchroom. Instead of having a lot of people inside, we want people to continue going outside in good weather, where it is healthier. Most people want to be sitting, looking out at the water. So we continue to keep up the large outdoor area with the Adirondack chairs. These are some of the good things that have come out of Covid.

CHAPTER 12

Working at the Bakery

GENERATIONS

Gael Watson

"I'VE KNOWN YOU SINCE YOU WERE JUST A BUMP IN YOUR MUMMY'S TUMMY." Honestly, I've known so many babies at that stage first—the bump. The bump that kept growing each week that I saw the mummy, and then, "Dun-dun-duuun!" Baby's born. And then, "Dah-dah-dahhh," working at the bakery. So many.

It's the neighbourhood people who came when they were in their twenties. They had children, and those children grew up, right from babyhood, being familiar with the bakery. Going to the bakery was something that they grew up doing, and I remember some of those kids, when they were six years old, saying, "I want to work at the bakery!" And sure enough, the day came, and they were working at the bakery. It's often a stepping stone for kids. It's a first experience of what that exchange of labour for money is. It's a bit difficult, to begin with, for them, because it's a steep curve to learn these things. But a lot of them don't find it to be a steep curve because they've been coming into the bakery their entire lives and they get it. They get what it is; I don't need to explain what it is. I might need to explain that they should look out for things to do when it's not busy, but I don't need to explain how they need to be with customers because they've seen it over the years. There's a lot of kids like that; they got to work at the bakery.

134

Kathryn Gordon

Gael hired all my kids when they were young. Desi was hired just to scrape potatoes and carrots. She did that for a while, then went on to bake. I don't know how long it took her, but she started at the age of thirteen. And then my daughter Sydney also started at twelve or thirteen years old and worked in the kitchen, bakery, and shop. Lily started young as well, and worked in the shop.

Peggy Greer

Many of my children worked for Gael. And that's a big part of the story for me. When I think of all those kids who got their kind of "boot camp" basic training at the LaHave Bakery, probably two generations now, really. Well that's pretty cool!

A RITE OF PASSAGE

Sadie Watson

I started working at the shop when I was eleven. Full days. I started working for $4.25 an hour, I think, and worked pretty much every weekend until I was eighteen or nineteen. I was always saving up for something. It more or less kept me out of trouble. I couldn't be hungover and come to work in the bakery.

Sadie Watson on the phone(s!) in the LaHave Bakery office, c. 1998. (UNKNOWN)

WORKING AT THE BAKERY 135

I—as a teenager—had to hold down my job. It was also in the family business, so I had to stay in line; probably a good thing! And then all of my friends came to work at the bakery. My best friends and I grew up here as teenagers. It provided income and freedom for so many of us. It was like a rite of passage to work here.

Nearly everybody needed, and had, a summer job. And working at the bakery, if you could nail it, was also fun. So: "Time to start earning my own money. I guess I'll go apply at the bakery." If you picked the bakery, it was more than likely that you had a sibling who went before you. There were the sisters, Tamara and Natasha; Zoë and Lucy Steele and their older sister Ona Archibald; and siblings Katherine and Kevin Knot.

SHOPKEEPERS, BAKERS, AND MORE

Gael Watson

We've got fifteen to twenty people on the payroll; more in the summertime. Some people work full-time; most people, twenty or thirty-five hours a week. In the office, there's myself, and then there's Laura, who's manager, and Andra, who works as a self-employed bookkeeper. We have two different people who work in the kitchen off the shop, because we're open seven days a week. In the shop, we have two or three shopkeepers, depending upon the season, making the espresso coffee, taking orders, and looking after the customers. Then you go down the stairs to the grocery store, and there's usually one person, sometimes two, working down there. If you go down more stairs, you go into three kitchens. The bread kitchen, sweets kitchen, and summer kitchen. There are two bakers working in the bread kitchen, one baker working in the sweets kitchen, and usually another person in the summer kitchen making sauces and getting ready for the take-home meals, doing the prep work for that. Making pizzas in that room. It used to be an extra kitchen, but now we're pretty much using it all the time. Then there's a person who delivers the bread three or four times a week. I think that's everybody.

LaHave Bakery staff, c. 1995. From left: Bernadette Corkum, Elenana Moore, and Donna Verge. (UNKNOWN)

Andra White

They'd come back each year—it was great. Students; often students. Some of them stayed; Laura and Erin are still here. A lot of them would move on. Gael would be happy for them. I think every one of them would say they really learned a lot by working here.

A ROOM WITH A VIEW

Gael Watson

The need for the staff room came about because the bakery started getting really intensely busy in the summers. There was nowhere for the staff to go. It is sometimes overwhelming to deal with the crush of hungry people, so it's important that the staff have a place to go for their breaks. After one particularly busy summer, I thought, "I've got to provide something." Staff would try going outside the building, but there would be people who would find them. There was nowhere to go.

At the very end of the building, facing the river, was a space. It was in the worst condition. It was starting to sag, and there was a lot of rot. It was pretty precarious, especially where it was over the water. Again, Rob Muise and Andrew Porter were called upon to tackle the job. That one corner was a decent-sized room, but it was a major undertaking to basically gut the area and go right down to the water level. New piers were put in and filled in with rocks. Heavy, heavy material was used. The floorboards in that room are three-inch planks, heavy planks, because everything that's over the water really needs to be double strength.

The repairs were made to that corner and it became the obvious place on ground level to put the staff room. We also put windows—all the windows—overlooking the water. A wonderful view. It's a private place, but it's also a really beautiful place to rest. It's heated. It's got a Persian rug, nice big couch, a little table, and there's a fridge and a microwave. That's the staff room. It's the secret room, because you have to go through the shop and through the "dungeon" area before you get to this other door that leads into this very comfortable sitting room.

APPLY WITHIN

Peggy Greer

Gael doesn't judge. She's open to people for who they are. Young people feel very comfortable around her. Everyone does. She gives people a chance. And the kids who work there are allowed to make mistakes.

Gael Watson

It's taken me a long, long time to know what to ask in an interview when somebody's applied for a job. I have come to realize that it's the personality—the person—and not necessarily the skill that they're bringing. It's nice if they have the skill. Usually, a skill can be inside somebody without them having worked for years at it. If you're good at multi-tasking, or if you're good at looking out for people, being a caring person, that's what I'm looking for. A person who cares.

I don't ask or expect that somebody sign their name on the dotted line and work for fifty years. I do look for people who really want to be a part of the bakery, who want that in their life now. But I'm really fine about people moving on, too. It's a natural thing to do.

I'll ask questions like, if they're young, what's their relationship within their family? Do they have pets? I want to know about their cats, if they grew up with animals. Cooking: "When did you begin to cook?" or "When did you begin to bake?" or "Why do you want to live here?" You can usually have a feeling that you can trust. Laura has become very much a part of the interviews. If an interview is working, it becomes quite a social event. You begin to have just an ordinary visit with somebody. During the course of that visit, it may be that the person you're talking to is now learning more about what the business is—what expectations we have, the history of the place, and where we're headed. They may think, "Nah, it's not what I want." Or they may be keen—really enthusiastic and keen.

I think, too, that the people who often end up staying with the bakery are people who have their own engine inside them. They're motivated. They don't need to be governed, because I'm not one to govern people. I don't want to shape somebody. I want them to find, within what we do, something that is enjoyable and challenging. I'm looking for individuals who are social, who can work with people. With a group, mostly of women, working together, of all ages, from fifteen through to—I'm the oldest one at sixty-eight.

I'm usually just as nervous as the person coming in. When it comes time for putting it out that we need somebody for a specific part of the business, it's really important that it's right for both sides. It has to be right for both sides. You need people who are able to see if the job is working for them, and saying something if it isn't. Because I don't want anybody to live a torturous life, biting their tongue. And it used to be that way. It was sort of an "us" and "them" kind of thing for a while. I really want to get away from that. I just don't want it in my life. I don't want to be the one that makes people shut up when I walk into the room.

It is, in fact, really hard to do what we do well, and to last from year to year to year. We need people who can think; really think in a multi-dimensional way. There's a lot to what the bakery is doing, and how it presents itself in the community. You're covering so many bases, in such a big building, with so many different things going on. The jobs here are more fluid, less "stop and start." A continuous flow that, I have found, women are just more adapted to. They've grown up to be that way. There have been men who have worked very well here, have been wonderful. But, I think, generally speaking, it's just very hard for a man in this kind of a business to feel natural in it. I'm very happy to interview men. It's always worth trying, because you want men to cut themselves out of that stereotype where they need to govern, where they want to do the telling and not the doing, when they rise and they puff themselves up and they think in some way they're superior to everyone else, including me. It hasn't worked.

Laura Pitts

I help Gael with hiring, which is really the most important part, I think, of our job. We really want to make it a good place to work, and the best thing that we can do is hire genuinely good people to work at the bakery.

LEARNING THE ROPES

Laura Pitts

One day, when we were closing the bakery, all of a sudden we were done. I said, "Oh my god, Erin. I think we just closed this whole bakery in fifteen minutes. I don't even remember doing it, it happened so quickly!" And she said, "How many times do you think we've closed this bakery?"

I started thinking about it. Hundreds. It got up to five hundred times. "We've closed this bakery five hundred times." So you can't expect somebody who's only closed the bakery three times to close it in fifteen minutes.

In my opinion, knowledge is power. If you share the knowledge around, you don't have to be responsible for everything; everybody is responsible. It's really important to have people empowered in their jobs and able to take control of a situation. Because I was the only full-time person working in the shop at the time, I didn't want to be the only person who knew things. I wanted everybody to be able to know. So—"Whoa! Why don't we make this list? Why don't we organize things?" So now, there are a lot of systems in place. Everybody can know what their job is, and there's an easy way to check if something's done. All that stuff has become really streamlined so everybody knows what's going on all the time, has the tools they need, and can voice their opinions.

Bev Kaulback

Bakers Linda Meisner (left) and Bev Kaulback in the bread kitchen, c. 2015. (UNKNOWN)

I believe in our bakery, and it is *our* bakery; we are not just employees. We all have a part in the bakery. The ones who trained me were trained by the ones before them, and it goes on and on and on. And then it came to me, and now I train the way I was taught. It's generations going right through the decades. It's amazing. And it all stems back to Gael because she's the one who started the bakery. She did the groundwork. She worked every position and section in that bakery to make it the success it is today.

WORKING TOGETHER

Peggy Greer

The bakery has always been a great place to work because there's a great sense of teamwork. When things get rolling in the high season and you get caught up in the ball that's rolling, that part is wonderful. Challenging, but mostly wonderful because of the pace. And joyful, too, and I think the joy goes into the food.

Gael Watson

Sometimes I'm alone in the office, but mostly I share it with the manager. Kathy Fisher was the first manager for the bakery. After Kathy died, Shelley Tracey became manager; we became good friends. She was fun, hard-working, and dedicated—a very nice person who stayed with the bakery for over ten years. Laura Pitts has been manager now for about eight years. She's really energetic and smart—a young woman who went to university and got her undergraduate science degree. She has chosen to live in the area. She started working at the bakery eleven years ago, as a student. She's been manager for about eight years. She's enthusiastic and comes up with great ideas. We often will put our heads together to figure out a dilemma that's happening. The nice thing about Laura is she's perfectly happy to, as I do still, go down and pack the bread, or roast the chickens, or clean a room out. She's involved in every part of what the bakery does, and, lately, with the grocery store.

Every Wednesday Andra comes in, and she's the bookkeeper. She sits at the middle desk. There are three desks: Laura's at one end of the room, I'm at the other, and Andra's in between. All our desks are on one side of the room so that, when the window opens, we all get the breeze coming in off the water. Andra is brilliant and we look forward to Wednesdays because we can catch up on everything that's going on in the bakery and outside of the bakery. She's been here for more than twenty years.

Laura Pitts and Erin Burke making Gael Watson's father's "Donald Robertson's Seville Orange Marmalade," c. 2012. (JANE MORRIGAN)

Andra White

It was an adjustment for me when I moved to Gael's office. I was used to having total silence in the little office, the bird room. But I liked sitting there with them, too. All of a sudden, you're seeing the inner workings of the bakery and what makes it tick, and it's a lot. It's busy. And then I got to know the staff. The staff would come up with questions, and I would see how Gael was pulled in a hundred—a thousand—different directions every day. And she just rolls with it.

Bev Kaulback

You go in, and Gael's motto—one of the things she says—is: "As long as you do your best, it's good."

Peggy Greer

I loved working there. It plucked me out of a dark place and I'm very grateful for that. Gael does that; she observes the community, and she reaches out. She's forever reaching out.

Gael Watson

If things go right, it's much easier, because you know why things are going well. It has to do with a lot of people going in one direction and thinking along the same lines, getting the same joke, or understanding the same loss. If something goes wrong, one person—and it needs to be me—is responsible. At the end of the day, I am responsible for things going wrong, just as much as partially responsible for things going right.

STAFF STORIES

Bev Kaulback

We have buckets of honey that we keep on top of our ovens to keep them warm so that the honey is liquefied. It was summer and hot in the kitchen—forty-something degrees. I went to take a bucket of honey down. I thought it was a full, new bucket, and usually the lid is on tight.

I didn't check. I took it down. The lid came off; the honey poured down over my head, all down my body, my shorts, my legs—everything. I thought, "Oh my god!"

I managed to save about a half a bucket. Then it was, "I have no clothes with me besides what I have on. I'm not finished work; I can't work." Gael happened to come down and see me. The look on her face was priceless.

"Oh my!" she said.

I said, "Don't worry. I've called Brian. He's bringing me clothes." I washed up and got all the honey out. I was a sweet person that day.

Gloria Barrett

Gael was very good to her people, no matter what. She always made sure they had money. She always put them first, and that's something that was new to me. I remember the first Christmas we had together. She took me aside and passed me a fifty-dollar bill, the pink one. I remember thinking to myself, "She can't afford it." But it really mattered to her that she took care of her little brood. We had a joke about that, from that point on. This fifty went back and forth between us about four thousand times. If she needed the fifty, there it was. If I needed it, I had it. Sadie needed it? "Okay, here's the fifty." I don't even know where it landed. I have no idea, but it was just this thing. And I was so impressed with that.

Andra White

I met Gael years and years ago when I would come for summer holidays. We decided to move here in 1996. Gael said she cried when she heard I was moving here, which was so sweet. After I'd been here for about six months, Gael needed a bookkeeper. I'd never been a bookkeeper, but I started doing bookwork for Gael. She was very patient because I was learning. It was great. That was in 1997, and I'm still her bookkeeper to this day—2021. That's like twenty-four years. Almost as soon as I started, I got pregnant, and Gael was so understanding about that. I used to bring my son to the bakery with me. When he was older, he would go with my mom. Then Wednesday was my day, coming to the bakery. It's always been my favourite day of the week. Wednesday's the bomb!

Laura Pitts

I started working there by chance. I think I was twenty-three years old. One day, the phone rang and it was Gael, who I'd only met a few times in my life. She said, "I had somebody who was supposed to work here this summer, and they can't come. I'm just wondering if maybe you'd be interested in working at LaHave Bakery?" Then she said, "I've already called Marion and asked her permission, and you can live with her."

And I said, "Well, okay then—sure. Why not?" And I thought, "Oh, great, I don't have to look for a job and I can spend the whole summer by the beach!"

So I worked there, and it was really hard work. It was very, very busy. The only jobs that I'd had up to that point were at the mall and I thought, "Oh, this is like Christmas at the mall." It was just throngs of people pressing up against the counter.

My first winter there was really exciting for me—to be in the building when it wasn't pressing. You get to know Gael more. You get to know the business more. You get to know all the regular customers.

When the manager left, I went up to the office and said to Gael, "I don't know if you need help, but I will be happy to help you with anything that you need." And Gael said, "Yes, one hundred percent," and cleared the desk off and sat me down.

I was like, "Oh, my god," and then I started learning about the inner workings of the business—and it was so great.

Bev Kaulback

In those first couple of hours in the morning, it's just you and that building and the silence. I like the silence. I like to listen to what's going on around me.

You hear every little creak of the wood and the floors—all the different sounds that you wouldn't normally hear with all the ovens going, machinery going, and people coming through, back and forth. For bread-making, we can take our breaks normally right at two hours. The bread has a life of its own. It demands our time, and that comes first. I usually try to gear my first break so I can go outside as the sun is coming up. I sit on the bench and watch the sky explode with colours over the water. It does something for your soul. Just those few moments for yourself. Then you go back in and it's—"Okay, a new day has begun. Get her done."

A few years ago, we had a wicked nor'easter. Knocked the power out. We still had the phones, so Gael and I were talking about the bake. I said, "Well, we can go over to the bakery." So we made bread the old-fashioned way, kneading by hand, on the counter. And we did muffins and scones. No Hobart. Just by hand, the two of us. I hadn't done that since I was twelve years old, when my grandmother taught me how to make bread.

We did rustic loaves. We kneaded and shaped the loaves and baked them in the propane ovens. It did turn out very good, but the labour was intense. It's amazing what the machinery does that replaces the human hand. I'm thankful for the machines, let me tell you! When we pump out all the bread that we do, there must be about five or six hundred loaves.

WOMEN SHINING

Gael Watson

I've had men working at the bakery who insist on calling us "girls." I've said to them, "We either go by 'women,' or you could use our names." Some become very apologetic and say, "It's very hard; I never know what to say."

I say, "It's easy; it's easy."

Laura Pitts

I had so much respect for Gael. I just couldn't believe that she was running this whole behemoth of a building and there was all this stuff going on in it. She would be there at the end of the day, when I was sweeping up or whatever, and telling me all these stories about the building and what it looked like at the start. I hadn't even heard of LaHave Bakery before in my life, so I was just totally enthralled, and was, "Oh my god. Who is this woman? She's doing it all."

I always envisioned I was going to live in the country. I told my mom when I was eight years old that I was going to buy a house and my husband was going to live in the house with me. So here, I felt like I could do it. And what was really interesting is that I found that the whole place is basically run by women. And I was—"This is amazing. This is my vibe." Women are running businesses. Cool! I'm in—big time.

I went to school and got this science degree where I learned all about environmental health, how plants grow, and how agriculture works. Then I moved here, and Gael's like, "Hi. I don't know anything about anything, but this is what I think." That's always the precursor with Gael. And I'm looking at her and—"Right, what you think is pretty sound here, Gael, and I'm on board." I'm on board with not putting chemicals in food, and I'm on board with making food that people can eat. I'm like, "Yes, yes, yes!" Also, I could work really hard at LaHave Bakery and ethically actually stand behind everything, which is amazing.

Kathryn Gordon

I've said to my daughter Desi, who was inspired by Gael and opened up her own bakery—Ploughman's Lunch—that sometimes the way she handles business reminds me of Gael. I think Desi really learned a lot from her. Not just baking, but business sense as well. Gael has influenced all my kids. Sydney learned the value of hard work. Lily, my youngest, also worked at the bakery. She was always working up front and she had a great time.

Gael always gives her staff the benefit of the doubt and cares about the people who work for her. She is an amazing human being. Very unusual. Even though she doesn't follow the normal course in business, she's an incredible businesswoman.

Laura Pitts

I feel very much it's 100 percent Gael's business—she's the boss; she's the final decision on everything. But I feel very heard and very open to throwing my ideas out there: "I think we should do this or that." I think Gael is the smartest, most amazing woman I've ever met in my life, to be honest. It's just crazy how brave she was.

When I turned thirty-two, she said, "That's how old I was when we bought this building." And I thought, "I would never, in a million years, ever buy that building looking how it was. Ever!" I never would have. It was so far out of my comfort zone.

I was like, "That's wild!" But here I was, standing in the business—the successful, famous LaHave Bakery—in this beautiful building, and Gael's like, "I'm going to open a bookstore." It was all just this expansion, and it was like, "Why can't I? Why can't I do it?"

It was so brave. She just went and did it. I think that's what I've learned from Gael. She makes decisions so quickly. It's great because she just trusts. Action—it's all about action with her, and it's really helped me in my life overall, just being around her all the time and having that forward motion. "Let's do it."

Bev Kaulback

It's that one-on-one time with Gael that is really beautiful. You get to know her a little deeper than what's on the surface, because I find Gael's very reserved. And the stories that she has—she has a lifetime of stories. She has endured so much. It is absolutely astounding what she has accomplished in a world that, not so much now—I mean, it's still there—but back then, was a "man's world." A lot of women weren't in business by themselves. She's been at this for, now, like thirty-five years, and the knowledge that she has is amazing.

Laura Pitts

We've all become a bit more vocal about equality of women and others in the past couple of years. It's been more prevalent in the media, and we've all been feeling a bit more that we can just say it, instead of just thinking it and keeping it in. "This business is run by a woman, and this whole business is running because of women." Gael often gets, "Can I talk to the owner? When is he going to be here?"

We're like, "No, it's run by a woman." The LaHave Bakery is full of very strong women. That's what we want. We want teenage girls, when they have their first job, to be surrounded by strong women—because we want them to be strong women. I think Gael, just by doing it in a very demure way—because she doesn't like to talk herself up—is leading us all by example.

CHAPTER 13

An Unconventional Business

A COMMUNITY BAKERY

Gael Watson

A LOT OF PEOPLE LIKE THE BAKERY; THEY LIKE IT AND THEY CHERISH IT. THE younger ones that have grown up with it, sometimes they'll get emotional about it, as it was to me. The bakery, the building, the history of it—it's just a wonderful thing to see it affecting other people in the same way.

Kathryn Gordon

It was Gael's bread—the taste, the quality—that attracted people to the bakery. And the lunches. That's what I remember. And just what she's done with the place and the lengths that she goes to support local people. There's always a lot of good energy with the staff. Young people attract more young people.

Laura Pitts

I became really close with Jesse and some of the other people that worked at the LaHave Bakery, including Anna Bald, Nicole Lynds, Erin Burke. We became a community of people who still are a community of people, ten years later, which is amazing. And the intergenerational hangout where everybody's coming together—like you and your kids and your mom and your grandparents are all at the same party. It was just something that was so unusual to me. I was in my early twenties; I thought it was so bohemian and tribal, and it was really intriguing—playing music and getting along. It was really a cool vibe; I just couldn't leave. The bakery itself was just like this magnet for that sort of feeling. It became sort of known during that time that if you were new into the neighbourhood, you want to come work at the LaHave Bakery, because that's where you met people in your age group. And you met the community in there.

Gael Watson

Ruby told me that LaHave used to have three banks, two garages, seven or eight stores, and a post office. When I asked Gloria what her house used to be, she said it was a general store but then it became a tinsmith shop. So it was a real village, and it was thriving, and it worked for the people, and they knew each other, and they talked to each other. I see that as being, you know—it may be a throwback in time, but I think we need to be nourished in that way again.

Peggy Greer

It has been a strange and wonderful journey watching the bakery become what it is. It started as a small community bakery and has become, really, a world destination. I have a friend who travels a lot. One time, he flew into Heathrow and had dinner in London at the house of a friend of a friend. They were having this lovely soup and my friend looked at a loaf of bread on the table and said, "That looks like LaHave Bakery bread!" The host said, "Yes, indeed it is. My friend just flew in from Nova Scotia and all I wanted him to bring me was LaHave Bakery bread."

THE CUSTOMERS

Gael Watson

I remember there was a woman, an older woman, who was always very cheerful and encouraging. I'm remembering there were elderly women who came to visit Ruby for tea who were great—women who were just very gentle, and they would come in regularly to buy a loaf of bread. There was one woman who would bring little gifts for Sadie.

This is something that all shopkeepers, if they've been shopkeepers for very long, feel the same about. The fact that you have people who come in for years, once a month or once a week. You never know their names; they know you, you know them, you have conversations. Sometimes you get their first names, but you're not close enough to them. The day they stop coming, you'll just wonder. "Wonder what happened to that person?" Sometimes, you hear they had a stroke, they're in a home. Emotion.

Sometimes, people will come. I'm thinking of a woman, really a lovely person. She got cancer. We used to see her out sailing with her husband. They came to the bakery and they were good regulars. And then she got cancer. She was going to win; she was going to get through it; she was going to fight it. And I saw that, as a shopkeeper: her waning health, but her spirit still going forward. And then one day she came in with a couple of women; they were her daughters. She came over to me and she said, "I'll say goodbye now." We hugged, and I knew I would never see her again.

I think a lot of the time the people who have come for all those years to buy bread at the bakery, it's enough for me that they love it, that they like it, and that they keep coming back. That it's part of their lives.

Bev Kaulback

In the wintertime, when it's a little slower, we don't see as many customers. We get to take a breather. On the nice winter days, we have people milling through all the time. All our personalities come out. We have our regular customers, which you can joke a little more with and have a little more fun with, and they get to know us as well. In the summer, there's people from wall to wall. You could go outside and there's cars lined on both sides of the road—and that's all you see. Don't get me wrong, it's beautiful. They're visiting us. That keeps us working.

Peggy Greer

In a way, for all of us working there, you had a short amount of training. Then, it was trial by fire because the mob—the customers—would arrive, and you would be facing, at times, fifty people waiting for a sandwich. You are making them one at a time. You don't look at the fifty people. You're looking at the one person you're making the sandwich for, and you give them the best service you can. You need focus and patience. I've always said, "If you can work at the LaHave Bakery, you could work anywhere in the world," because you have that basic training of focussing, and one-on-one, and get the job done. "Next! Can I help you?"

EQUALITY

Gael Watson

Right from the very beginning, I have—I just believe in equality. I want equality. I never thought it would be a hard thing to achieve, and we still have such a long, long way to go to become equals to each other—for everybody to be as important as the next person. Still, if you keep it in mind that that's what you're aiming for, then you can make adjustments. For me, I've had that opportunity of being able to stay around, stay in the game, for a long, long time. So you can make these little adjustments that are not even noticeable. You're learning; you're seeing what went wrong. You're seeing how things work on a very minute, day-to-day basis. It's worth it if we can ever become equals; it will always be worth it.

I would like to always be the one who does the filthiest jobs, the most tedious things, to be the last one finishing something up. I would like to be that person, and often I am. If it's a really dirty toilet situation, I'm down there. Also, I want to teach myself that it is something important to always be willing to confront situations, personal situations, with somebody who works at the bakery. Nobody likes confrontation but, inevitably, I'm the one who will need to say something—to find a way to say something that isn't going to destroy myself or the person.

That's been very challenging. And, in terms of being equal, it's important to learn that failure isn't something that sticks on you all the time—that everybody fails, and to accept that—just as when we've made something and it works; when we've had a really wonderful encounter with a customer; when we've made it to the end of the day and we're still laughing. Those things really help make you feel like you can have equality. You can have this sense that we're all breathing the same air. We're all still wanting to feel at the end of the day, "That was a good day." Or, if it wasn't a good day, that we were all suffering through it together.

I think that, over the years, I've found that it's a mistake to make anybody the "head" something or another. There is a tendency, sometimes, to feel that they no longer need to do the grunt work—to wash the dishes, or wash the dishes but not the pots. "Somebody else can finish up. Somebody else that has less seniority should finish up." I don't like that. I don't think that's right. I think that no matter how many years you've been working in a job, you should always be one of the people that washes up and fills containers and does a little bit before turning the light out at the end of the day.

Peggy Greer

Gael will give anyone a chance and treat them like an equal. It's hard, because she does often seem superhuman, and works way too hard, in my estimation. This is intimidating in a way because you think, "Why can't I do that?" And she doesn't even realize it; she doesn't realize that she is an amazing person, a "Wonder Woman."

KEEPING IT REAL

Peggy Greer

Well, from my perspective, I believe it works because she keeps it on the ground. She knows that at any moment the ground will shift, but she's steady on her feet and low to the ground. She has her own style and that is sometimes challenging to accountants and bankers. She does it by feel, by instinct, and she's good on those feet. If you think of this grocery shop as an example, her timing is brilliant, but she never lets things lift her off her feet. Her style is, "I'm here, I mean to do business, and I'm going to get 'er done." Gael has never been big-minded. She is who she is and has consistently remained who she is.

Laura Pitts

Gael's way of doing things is very, very straightforward. It's not like, "Let's have a meeting about marketing." We're doing marketing by having that yellow colour for the label. That's marketing. I don't think Gael ever sat down and thought, "Oh, how am I going to market this?" She just did it. There's no weird veiling or any terminology connected to it. It's just—money comes in, and then money goes out again. We need to get money in so we can pay these bills. This is how much things cost. It's really straightforward: "All I have to do is this." Invoicing, bookkeeping—everything is just sort of how you would run your own house income, except it's the income of this giant building.

Gael Watson

One point about modern food production in large plants has always been the level of keeping an eye on things. I learned by experience, with the Mahone Bay outlet, that I'm much smarter with what's under my nose. I wasn't acknowledging that, at every move, I was making adjustments in LaHave; always making adjustments. When I was on the *Selchie*, out on the ocean, trying to run things in LaHave and Mahone Bay, I found I really struggled. My brain was working differently. To a lesser degree, when I was in LaHave and running Mahone Bay, it was the same problem. I couldn't get my head around it. Therefore, I can see how things can be overlooked that are important; I can see how it happens. Change can't happen fast enough, because you're not close enough. You're not there. So I think modern production needs to get into smaller units in order for us all to be safer. It's healthier.

I feel that the only way I can have a daily grasp of all of the various things we do is to be the only one who writes the paycheques once a week and pays the bills. It's a good practice, because every time I write a person's name, I think about that person—how important they are. How is it going with them; the work that they do; what they bring in personality and skills; what they need; what part they play in the working of the bakery. It's a reminder, physically writing out the cheques. It reminds me about how much money we're spending. I can recognize really easily, because of that, if something is off. It's very basic, but it works; it works for me.

Gael Watson working through the night in the LaHave Bakery office, c. 1986. (UNKNOWN)

Andra White

Gael always made payroll. She always had the bakery open, even on days when I would see the daily sales—because I would tally them—were forty dollars. She always met payroll. When you look back, you see how hard it was, but she never lost faith. She would just come every day and do it. And then, slowly but surely, she started chipping away at all of that debt, and chipping away and chipping away. The bakery started growing.

So much happens in a day of Gael's life. Holy cow—how can she remember everything without making a list and scratching things off the list? It's been fun observing. I wouldn't have missed it for anything. Nothing.

Peggy Greer

That's the whole thing. Gael's not especially interested in profit. She's not greedy; she's generous. Perhaps to a fault. It's not about making a big profit. For her, it's the dream, the journey. It's about—"keep it moving, keep it on the road, you can do this, just keep it going." That's how it's been for all these years. So that's pretty cool.

A LIVING WAGE

Gael Watson

There's something called the Canada Living Wage, which has been determined, on average [in 2021], to be twenty dollars an hour. I think it's a little less in Nova Scotia, but I'm looking at twenty dollars. If you can earn twenty dollars an hour, you will be able to; unless you have bad habits, you should be able to pay for decent food and lodging. Twenty dollars is the bar that's been set. The bakery is a business where the only place we get our money is not from what we make, but what we sell, and it's perishable. So there's a timer on everything we make. We can get our raw ingredients in, but once we've turned it into bread or food, then the timer is on. The chance of losing it, or certainly an amount of it, is there, always. It's always been, and continues to be, a challenge to pay decent wages and, at the same time, source quality ingredients and make our food affordable.

This is my dilemma. It's a very limited amount of actual money coming in from the bread to pay those wages and keep up with the overhead. We started making the take-home dinners, which are frozen, and that, for sure, has really helped. It has more time to sell.

The goal, right from the very beginning of opening the grocery store, was the living wage—being able to get to twenty dollars an hour. Because more money is coming into the grocery store, I'm placing a lot of anticipation that it will, in turn, mean that the people who work at the bakery will be able to earn better wages. We're definitely making progress towards that end. That's really nice, to be able to voluntarily go beyond the minimum increase, and the grocery store is making that happen. In addition to that, if somebody's really working well and helping that end goal, then there are bonuses. There's recognition for going the extra mile. A lot of people at the bakery do that. It's really noticeable.

Laura Pitts

We've been really focusing, the last couple of years, on paying our year-round, long-term staff, trying to get them to that twenty-dollars-an-hour mark. We want them to be making a living wage. So we're looking at how we're going to make more money so we can give those staff members who are amazing more money. And then you're getting closer and closer and closer, and you're like—okay, okay, we're almost there; we're almost there.

Then you start thinking, of course, bigger. We're all working off Gael, so then you start thinking even bigger. "Well, what else? Could we maybe get benefits? Do you think that we could maybe get dental?" And then you're like, how much more money will we have to make to do this? Could we be a small business in rural Nova Scotia who pays benefits? Hopefully. Hopefully. That's what we want. That's our goal, because it's not about making a whole bunch of money; to sit on a pile of money. We want to get the money so that we can better the world. You can have a job that is totally safe, year-round, reliable, in rural Nova Scotia, where you're totally respected as a human being, you don't have to sacrifice your ethics, and you can also have dental. What kind of world is that? But it's the world that we could try for.

RUBY'S HOUSE

Gael Watson

Ruby, who lived to be 104, never wanted to sell her house. She loved her little house, and she was able to have it for most of her life. It was after she died that I asked her nieces if I could buy it. My thinking was, at the time, that this has become an area where ordinary people can't really afford to buy the houses along the shore. It was getting harder and harder for people who would like to work at the bakery to find a place to rent. That was a growing dilemma, and still is. "Where am I going to live? I'd like to work there." I was buying the house, and that's what it is. It's affordable housing for people who work at the bakery. We've said, "You need to be able to work three days a week at the bakery in order to live in Ruby's House." We've had the house now for three or four years—three years anyway—and it's worked very well. It's been a great place for people to live. It's right on the water. It's a really nice little house. And it's still called Ruby's House.

When Ruby married Lawrence in 1937, they moved into that house. It was a garage, originally. The earliest pictures I have, have got that house in it. So it was probably built in the early 1900s. At one time, it had a barber shop on one side. Andrew Porter and Rob Muise were once again the carpenters, restoring it and making it into a comfortable and strong house. When it was being renovated I went down into the cellar. Standing and looking at the work, I looked up at the ceiling. I thought, "What am I looking at?" and I realized that it was a ship's mast as the main beam holding that house. That's what we found. It's absolutely solid, still supporting the house—so appropriate for a little house by the mouth of the river, being supported by a schooner's mast.

UPSTAIRS, DOWNSTAIRS

Gael Watson

There's always been a lot of people who worked at the bakery. A lot of people, a lot of personalities. For years and years and years, there were the "downstairs people"—the people who worked through the night baking bread or making the sweets, and the "upstairs people"—the shopkeepers. Because they worked separate shifts through the night and through the day, there was always a tendency to blame one or the other. There was always an opportunity to say, "Oh well, you know, it's the people upstairs," or "It's the people downstairs, ha ha."

When we made the adjustment to everybody overlapping each other, so that everyone knew each other, things improved. Both the "upstairs" and the "downstairs" people began to see what the other was doing. They could see, "Oh, you know, there is a lot of work going into making this bread," and "Oh, there's a lot of stress involved in dealing with crowds of people who are hungry." Both sides, occupations, began to have a more compassionate view of the others. So that was a really good move. You have to remember that I had no idea how to do anything, in terms of having things working out well, with the number of people that were doing different things. It took a while to shake these things out; to realize that that would improve the shifts.

We went for over fifteen years baking through the night. Really, the change wasn't in order to bring people together and make them understand each other and have good relations. That wasn't the reason; that wasn't the thing that changed it. It was that there were fewer and fewer people who were willing to work through the night. It's hard on the head to start work at nine o'clock and run through the night until five in the morning. But I'd been doing it all along, so my initial feeling was, "What's wrong with people? I could do it." Until one day I thought, "All right then, let's start later. Let's start at four o'clock in the morning instead of nine o'clock at night. What it meant was that everybody was able to get a decent night's sleep. Your life is still fairly balanced, and your body is balanced with the time. So the beginning for resolving the problem was really only because I couldn't get people to work through the night!

PAPER BAG

Gael Watson

Well, there were people who certainly told me that I couldn't run my business. They didn't exactly tell me what I should be doing—"this would be better, that would be better." In fact, there were times when I was told, in no uncertain terms, that that person could do better with a paper bag over their head than what I was doing.

On a few occasions—I would say maybe ten occasions over the long period—people were feeling that I wasn't being fair or I wasn't doing enough. There was one time when I had a load of gravel dropped and spread in the driveway so that it wasn't muddy. That was a problem. One person felt that the money could have gone into better wages. So there were things like that. It's just the kind of a calculation that is always done when a person who works for you sees you spending money and disagrees with where that money should be spent. It all should go into wages and nowhere else—not seeing the picture of making the place so that people are happy to come in and feel that it's safe to be there. In order to encourage people to feel comfortable, that the food is good, you need to put money in places where you can make that obvious. That you're looking out for everyone. Rebuilding the stairs to make them stronger and safer—jobs like that would sometimes come into criticism.

There were times, you know, I took it to heart, criticism. You have to take it in, and you can't be defensive when somebody is really upset. Whether they can articulate exactly what's making them unhappy, you still need to take it home and consider whatever they've said. Often, there are parts of it, not all of it, but parts of it, that can make you feel that you can do something. Criticism can often be moving forward. Sometimes it has led to my finding out there can be something better. Someone has a problem, and you think, "Well, is there anything we can actually do about this?" And often there *is* something you can do about it.

Criticism is hard to take, but you need to receive it in silence and not just push back. That's something I've learned: that you can't just be offended, because it doesn't really matter what somebody is saying to you. It's the fact that they are not happy. You have to consider what's behind it. There are many, many times that a person is unhappy, not necessarily because of the work, or the workplace, or me. It's something that's happening in their lives, and it's making it difficult for them to have a job at the bakery.

APPRECIATION

Laura Pitts

The thing that I really liked about the job, that made me come back every summer, is that Gael really made me feel like—I'm going to get emotional here—but she really made me feel like I was appreciated. I worked really hard, but I also was really appreciated by her. I felt acknowledged for hard work which, in the world, doesn't happen. Working there doesn't pay a whole bunch of money, but there's so many other benefits to it. You feel heard. You feel seen. Gael really cares about people, and she really cares that people can have a life here.

Bev Kaulback

When Gael arrives, first thing she does is come down to say good morning. She will acknowledge us: "Good morning. How is everybody today? How are things going?" It's really nice. And then she'll look and she'll say, "Bread looks beautiful." That little pat on the back really goes a long way. You know she appreciates everything you do every day. And we appreciate her every day.

After we put in a wicked summer with all the heat and we worked really hard, Gael would give us a summer bonus. When you open the envelope and you're seeing this, it's like, "Wow!" I had never had that anywhere else in my working life. It was a show of appreciation of all the hard work that we had done. Last summer, we were at Gael's residence. She had table snacks out and beverages and everything to say, "Job well done." Everybody came and sat and talked and laughed and ate. It was really nice.

Gael would give us a bonus in the wintertime as well, especially if it was a really hard winter. She'd always do a little something for you. Another thing Gael does for us is that every second shift we get a free loaf of bread. And then, my first year, when we had our Christmas party, we went upstairs and into the gallery—beautiful room. She had the meal catered, and there was wine and beverages and everything there. Music if we wanted music. Usually Jesse had music going in the background, a little low, and on the table would be a present. Gael goes to every employee and thanks them for attending and working at the bakery and wishes us a merry Christmas. There's nothing fake about it. It's honesty with her, all the way. I find that there's a lot of genuine love for Gael. We collect money every year for Gael's birthday and purchase a present for her. And she's floored that we do it—every time. She can't believe that someone would think of her that way when she thinks of us that way all the time. Gael goes above and beyond for all her staff. Always has.

Peggy Greer

Grateful and generous is just what Gael is. She's so grateful to those who've worked with her, and generous in thanking them over the decades. She is kind, open, and willing to give people a chance. And then, if you step up to the challenge, she's extremely grateful—and shows it.

PART 4
Past, Present, Future

CHAPTER 14

Glimpses into the Past

SOU'WESTER

Gael Watson

IT'S AN AMAZING, HUGE, HUGE BUILDING, GOING ON AND ON. IN MY EARLY MEMories of coming to the LaHave Outfitters store with my family in the 1960s, I don't remember the fish plant in operation there. I remember the smell—the oil and machine smell in an unheated building. Fish boxes piled up.

I remember going into the store long before we owned it. Teleen was there in his rocking chair. He stood up and went behind the counter. I said, "I'd like to buy a sou'wester."

"Certainly!" He put on his hat, put on his coat, got his white cane, walked out the door. I watched him go down the road to Creaser's where they made fishing gear, rain gear. Then he came back again, right behind the counter, with a new sou'wester.

"That'll be fifteen dollars."

The Robertson children walking down a ramp from the Bluenose II *construction at the Smith & Rhuland shipyard in Lunenburg, 1963. From left: Leigh, Kim, Jane, and Gael.* (DONALD ROBERTSON)

"HOW OLD IS IT?"

Gael Watson

People ask me about the building all the time: "How old is it?" Well, it was built in 1901 by Boehner Bros. of West LaHave for Laughlin Currie. So the building is 120 years old, and Laughlin Currie was the original owner.

Fraser and Mabel (Wile) Gray's seven sons, c. 1925. Back row, from left: Lawrence, Eliot, Marvin, Teleen. Front row, from left: Fenwick, Mark, Webster. (UNKNOWN)

"Outfitting" is outfitting the ships with all the provisions—food provisions for the crew as well as ropes and chains, fishing gear, and anything that a boat would need for a voyage. The LaHave Outfitting Company shop had for sale in it all these things and more. In the back of the building, initially, the first floor was a fish plant, where they salted, cured, and dried cod. The two upper floors were for salt storage as well as multiple provisions.

The building was built very strong to hold the salt—with those strong, heavy timbers. Basic, basic carpentry, except in the shop, which is glorious with its tongue-and-groove panelling, high tin ceilings, and the solid brass cash register. The oak cabinets. It was a beautiful showpiece, as so many of those shops were.

The LaHave Outfitting Company building, as seen from the river, c. 1960, showing its deteriorating condition. (Unknown)

The original wharf, I think, was well over a hundred feet long. They had a rail line out to the end, where there was a smokehouse.

It wasn't the heyday in the thirties, and Fraser Gray was getting older. He was born in 1874, and he wanted to retire. He had correspondence with a lawyer by the name of Robertson, from Bridgewater, and he's writing to him saying he wants to sell out, sell up, get out of business. Robertson writes back and says, "Yeah, sure, no problem. All you need to do is pay out your shareholders." It was all about shareholders in those days and, of course, there was no money to pay out the shareholders. So in his early sixties, Fraser Gray turned around, walked across the road to the Royal Bank, and got a loan to buy this Fairbanks Morse diesel engine and compressor. He started up again, this time freezing fish. They went from salting and curing fish from the Western Banks and sending it down to the Caribbean in trade for salt, to freezing fish and selling it in Nova Scotia and west to Ontario and further west. I have pictures of the LaHave Fish trucks that belonged to the LaHave Outfitting Company. That was the shift, in 1935. I would say their fish business finished by the end of the sixties.

There were seven boys in the Gray family, but you only hear of Fraser Gray and two of his sons, Teleen and Lawrence—only those three Grays—involved in that building. But it appears that it was a fairly successful business for a long time, until the 1960s. Around 1963, I think, it started to waver.

OLD RECORDS

Gael Watson

Before the building was sold to us, Teleen and Lawrence Gray gave almost all the paperwork and a lot of the equipment and interesting pieces of that period—the turn of the twentieth century—to the Maritime Museum of the Atlantic in Halifax, as well as the Nova Scotia Archives. The history of the building I got through papers that were left behind. The old receipts gave me an idea of what the business was. The receipts that were left in the building were what had been shoved underneath things; I gathered together crumpled bunches here and there. Because it was a dark building with very few windows in the back, they weren't able to get all of it. I got the rest of it and started compiling and putting it into chronological order. I got a feel for what was being moved around

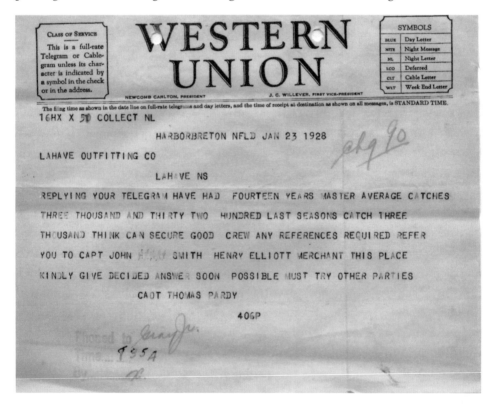

A telegram from Captain Thomas Pardy of Harbour Breton, NL, to the LaHave Outfitting Company, c. 1928—one of the many documents found in the building and archived by Gael Watson.

and what kinds of things would be bought—what people were looking for, what people were buying, what they were selling. And there was a daily packet boat, the *Atlantic*, out of Halifax, moving grocery items and provisions. Everything, before the roads were good, was by freight, coming in and out of the wharves. Water freight.

The old papers would talk about how much fish; how many tons of fish. The knowledge of where to find the fish was important. It's been a while since I looked at them. It was like the old cookbook, being able to touch these things knowing that they were the workings of ordinary daily life at the turn of the twentieth century. It's pretty wonderful, really, to have that close contact with an actual piece of paper from that time.

I still have a number of the old telegrams. The telegram was the way to communicate, before the telephone, on a daily basis, let's say. Fraser Gray would be looking for seafarers for the fishing boats or cooks or various people that they needed. There's a wonderful wealth of telegrams back and forth between Harbour Breton, Newfoundland, and LaHave Outfitters. There's correspondence back and forth talking to somebody who is applying to be skipper. He talks about what his record is for finding fish and hauling fish. There are negotiations looking for crew, looking for cooks. There are other telegrams that are just between short distances, LaHave and Lunenburg, talking to other schooner owners about the deals they've made and their negotiations, about picking up cargo, dropping off cargo. These telegrams really give you an idea of day-to-day life and the way things were. The speed of it, the daily sending of telegrams, was pretty efficient.

SALT FOR SALT FISH

Gael Watson

In the early days, places that had access to the ocean—especially close access, as the LaHave River did—were very, very busy. Places such as LaHave and Riverport and Fort Point. There are pictures of huge multi-masted schooners that would come and go, and small-masted boats, too, that would come and go. At one point there were, I think, hundreds of ships that came and went out of LaHave. There was a customs office in LaHave. By the time the early thirties came, there was obviously the downturn everywhere.

The trade was salt fish. A large and successful company called Black Bros. had a huge fish-processing plant on the Fort Point in the early 1900s. This big plant had a really long wharf. Different people have said it was two hundred feet long. It was also used as a steamship wharf, which means bringing big boats in. You can see the remains of this wharf jutting way out into the water, even to this day, in low tide.

The islands the LaHave Outfitting Company dealt with were the Turks and Caicos in the Caribbean. There were a lot of schooners, and they were all co-owned by people in the community. There was rarely, at least in LaHave, a boat that was owned only by one person. These schooners would go out to the Western Banks, and they would fish for cod. They'd come in, the cod would be cured, then the same schooners would take on the finished product—the salt cod—and they would go down to the Caribbean. They would first go down to Puerto Rico to off-load the cured fish. Then they went to the Turks and Caicos to on-load the salt, which was poured directly into the hold of the ship.

Salt was like gold. Salt was everything in the days before refrigeration. Curing food with salt, the salt was used for almost everything. So that was the trade that Lawrence Gray explained to me. "Salt for salt fish."

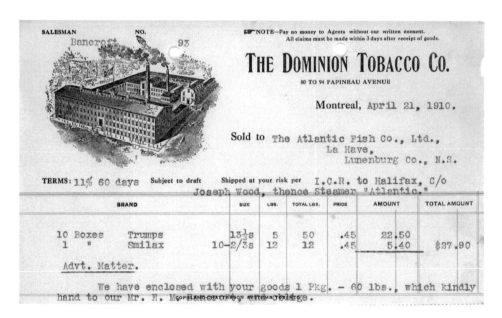

One of the many old invoices Gael Watson found in the LaHave Bakery building in 1985.

THE *JUTLAND* LOST AT SEA

Gael Watson

Fraser Gray was one of the *Jutland*'s shareholders. That's why I have all the paperwork for the *Jutland*—the survey, the bills from Boehner Bros., and the registration of it. The *Jutland* had a crew of twenty-one. It wasn't its first trip, but the second or third trip of fishing; it left from Halifax and was never seen again. I have the casualty report for twenty-one men lost. There was never any understanding of what had happened.

The interesting thing about the *Jutland* is that it's the story of many boats that went out with a crew of twenty or so people and never returned. That crew was from all over Nova Scotia, but most were from Liverpool, Nova Scotia. I think that instead of losing an entire village community from one place, they tried to have it so not everybody from that community was on one boat. But that used to happen—entire communities, all the men and boys were gone. It was perilous; it was a perilous life, fishing.

OLD STORIES

Gael Watson

When it came to getting history, the history of LaHave, it was a little scant. That was when I learned that just because you're old doesn't mean to say you're interested in history. People would never actually sit down and tell stories about how things went. Thinking back, I never really had time to ask the questions and hear the stories. Isn't that just the way? And when you do, then it's too late; people have grown old and memories fade. So, on and off, I would get anecdotal glimpses of the history of the way things used to be. But there were specific things I asked about. Like, in the beginning with Lawrence's father, Fraser, who bought the building, Lawrence could tell me about those first decades. Lawrence was responsible, from 1935 on, for keeping the generator, the engine, and the compressor going, which would pump ammonia through for the super-frozen freezer rooms for freezing fresh fish.

It was always in conversation that someone would mention something. Ruby Gray told me about the fire that burned down the Black Bros. fish plant at Fort Point. "My mother," she said, "knew who it was." They lived right on the Fort Point Road. Ruby told me the story that her mother, Vera, was in the kitchen when, one day, as it was getting dark, she saw a man and recognized him. He was going out toward the plant, and he was carrying gasoline. He ignited a massive fire that burned that huge building to the ground. Her mother would never tell because she was afraid for her own house. In her whole life, she never told Ruby who it was, but Ruby told me on more than one occasion that her mother knew exactly who it was, and that it was arson.

One day I said to Ruby, "Gosh, you know, Riverport is known for rum-running." I'd see the big houses there, but I'd look at houses in LaHave and they're pretty nice, too. So I asked her, because this was her time—she's from LaHave—"What was going on in LaHave, what about LaHave?" Her only answer to me was, "Well, Gael, we had our advantages." So in other words, if I wanted to know more, I was going to have to find it out for myself.

There was a terrible fire down by where the ferry is now in 1957. The whole low end of the street burned up. It was accidently started in Creaser's oil-clothing store, down toward the ferry. I've been told it was caused by a pop machine dispenser that short-circuited. It burned down the store and several houses, a sail loft, and a barber shop as well.

Sadie Watson

Ruby and Lawrence Gray were really of this community. They told me lots of stories about what it was like seventy or eighty years before. They'd lived through the Depression. They saved all their pie plates and Lawrence would fix the roof of the house and the garage with them. For me, they were my personal touchstone to the Depression years and how frugal they were. They'd lived through Prohibition; rum-smuggling days. Lawrence told us the story of how he'd run rum up to Bridgewater in his Model T Ford.

One story was a funny story. Lawrence always said he owned the first Model T Ford in the LaHave River Valley, that it arrived in a crate and he built it here at the building. He'd burn around. Sometimes he'd drink and drive. One day, he came screaming down the hill from the church, in the direction of the post office.

He went off the road across from the post office and crashed into the river. He said people were so upset with him, apparently, that nobody would help him. So he had to take the car, piece by piece, out of the river and rebuild it. It was, "Everyone's gonna teach Lawrence a lesson for dangerous driving." There were stories like that, that he would tell.

Open doors, and a community. Ruby and Lawrence were a connection to a different time. Another story was they would skate on the river all the time. When I was a kid, we had an icebreaker going up and down the river, so we would never skate out onto the river. But before the icebreaker was moving through, when they were growing up and into their adult years, they would skate. Lawrence would say he would skate across to Riverport. I can't imagine that happening now, in terms of the climate. That river does not freeze now, and I can't imagine that I'll see it frozen again. Interesting things like that—that would give this perspective, life on the river, how it's changed. I remember Ruby talking about how when she was a little girl, the ferry used to cross much further up the river, I think in West LaHave. There was an ice road that the cars would cross over on. She must've been a very young woman for the time frame—maybe a teenager. Anyway, a car crossed either too early or too late in the season. They were skating on the ice, and the car went through. She told me about the haunting headlights, shining up through the ice, and there was nothing they could do as this car went down near the middle of the river.

It's the stories that are gone. They go with the people. All of those stories were part of my upbringing.

CHAPTER 15

LaHave Today

RESURGENCE

Kathryn Gordon

IN THE LAST FIVE YEARS, THERE HAS BEEN A RESURGENCE OF YOUNG PEOPLE BUYING old buildings and turning them into corner stores or food-related industries.

Gael Watson

A lot of people were buying houses who weren't living here. In the late '90s, early 2000s, things began to change. There were more people moving in. But there was always that threat that the schools—Petite [Rivière Elementary School] and Pentz [Elementary School]—were going to be closed down. That all the kids were going to be shipped to a bigger school in, say, Bridgewater.

So it wasn't really opening up. It didn't have that feeling until the schools were secured. And then, in the last few years, it really has changed. Of course, with the pandemic, a lot of people have wanted to move to the country, realizing they can run their businesses from rural areas. I think that is a good trend in LaHave itself. There's been three or four houses sold where people have moved in, just in the last couple of years. Phew! That's what you want. You want people to live in your community. You don't want great passages along the road where you just see dark houses because they're waiting for that week, or two weeks, for their summer people to visit. It's just much more balanced lately.

LAHAVE IN 2021

Gael Watson

When you cross the river on the ferry, from east to west, you come to LaHave proper. The ferry is great—having that connection with the other side of the river. The distance coming from Lunenburg is shortened by half. It's a shortcut to LaHave, but also a lot of people like to take the trip and then carry on to the beaches. So LaHave Bakery is in a very good position.

The ferry's been there for a very long time; for over one hundred years. Jesse has a wonderful picture of the older ferry in his office. They're rowing a horse and carriage across, further up the river in West LaHave where the first ferry was that crossed the river. It was this big, long boat, and there's the horse, standing there, docile as can be with the cart, crossing the river.

LaHave Seafoods opened the same year as the bakery did, in 1985. It's a major business in LaHave. That is the other building that has had commerce in it for over a hundred years, just like the LaHave Outfitting Company building, where the bakery is. At one time, there was a grocery store in it, which I do remember as a child—going into the Red and White. The Himmelman family has owned the building all those years. LaHave Seafoods is run by David Himmelman and his son Ryan. When they were bringing fish in, they would process that fish in LaHave. Now, they own a scallop dragger. They go out to sea for two weeks and are in for two weeks. They come back with very large scallops, which are shucked and frozen at sea. That's where we get our scallops from. Ryan brings a 50-pound sack over his shoulder, and walks across the grass to the bakery. We turn those scallops into scallop pies, as well as sell them in our grocery store.

Gloria Barrett has been right here in LaHave for all these years, painting every day still. She's had her studio and shop for over forty years, selling handmade and eclectic things—everything from rugs from her friend who lived in Egypt to her wonderful paintings.

Vaughan Smith and Jackie Cohen have Westcote Bell Pottery and Artworks. They've been here now for ten years or so; they are really nice people. They actually came in and asked me: they said that they were interested in buying the property next door, that they were potters and Jackie's an artist and, "How would you feel about that?" I was amazed that they would ask. It was a smart move too, because we do have businesses next to each other. They said that part of the reason for deciding on LaHave was because of the bakery. The bakery did, in fact, attract that business, and they're wonderful people. They have a great pottery shop and gallery and, up until Covid, they taught pottery.

Down the road, in West Dublin, there's Desi Gordon with her bakery, Ploughman's Lunch. Desi makes wonderful pastries and sourdough bread—and that's great. She had worked at the bakery for a number of years when she was a teenager. She went to Montreal and learned more about pastry making. Desi and her husband, Stefan Kirkpatrick, bought this little old store in West Dublin. It's a really nice business in an old building. Everyone does things differently; there's room for lots of people with their ideas. If you are going to take on the responsibility of starting a business, you might as well do it your way, and that's what they're doing. When people ask for sourdough bread, it's great to be able to say, "Well, if you just keep on driving about five minutes down the road, there's a wonderful little bakery that makes sourdough bread and delicious pastries." It makes it a very mutually good thing.

Opposite the ferry, right beside the LaHave Fire Department, Susan Babe has her antiques shop. She sells antiques, homemade furniture, folk art, old books, and old tools.

Paul Kelly is an artist—a super-realist artist. He paints and draws. He and his family also make little wooden boats, model airplanes, whales, and other carvings that they sell in the summer at their little pop-up business next to Ruby's house. Also, there's another studio and gallery, with a jeweller and a sculptor, in the village.

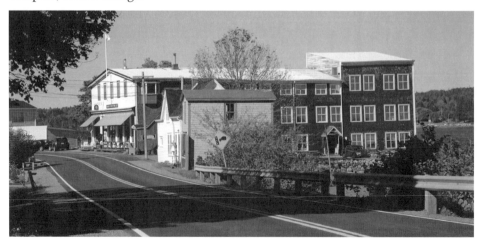

The LaHave Bakery building, as seen when approaching from the south on Route 331, c. 2021. (Jane Morrigan)

MAKING A DIFFERENCE

Kathryn Gordon

Without a doubt, the LaHave Bakery brought business to LaHave—and tourists. I think it attracted the pottery shop. I think the bakery probably attracted the jewellery shop. There's an antique shop there now, too. The ferry is right there. And Gael, you know, when Gael went out on that bakery boat, I think they really brought a lot of attention to the bakery. But it's a famous location now. And every year it gets bigger and better.

Gael was ahead of her time. It's the food, the building; it's the location. It's the way Gael has designed the eating areas—what she's done outside with the chairs, brightly painted yellow. She's just got an eye for this retail thing. She knows what she's doing with her Old World aesthetic.

Gloria Barrett

Oh Lord. The bakery, now, makes an incredible difference in life for so many people. Innumerable. They come from everywhere. Everybody knows about the place. Everybody wants to be part of it. Everybody is so excited. You know, if she was to pull up stakes right now, have a heart attack, close the door—everybody would be devastated. I don't know what they would do.

Anyway, it's a real place in the community. If it was a supermarket, they'd say, "It's our anchor store." Well, it is an anchor store. Gael wanted to have more and more things. It was wonderful.

Peggy Greer

And to see what it's become, with the gallery, the skateboard floor, the bookstore, the craft co-op, the marina, and now the grocery shop—it's pretty incredible.

Andra White

Always that same feeling, you know? I mean, lots of changes, but always that same feeling in the bakery. Just walking in, that beautiful, warm, delicious smell, lovely music, bright sun, cheerful staff—for the most part. Even though it's expanded so much, it's just got that beautiful feeling of a place you want to be around.

Sadie Watson

I think the bakery and the building continue to be a focal point in the community, and they play a really important role in how the community has continued to form and shape and develop.

CHAPTER 16

An Eye to the Future

PRIORITY ONE

Gael Watson

THE WHARF, WHICH IS SO IMPORTANT TO THE BUILDING, NEEDS TO BE REPAIRED. It's been taking a lot of abuse as the sea slowly rises. Unlike a couple of decades ago, now when we have storms coming from the northeast the waves not only hit the wharf really hard, but they go right over it. The pure weight of that much water striking the wharf is pushing it, and causing the underpinnings of it to break down, so that it's breaching right now. It's breaching at the bottom, and the rocks that are inside the wharf are spilling out. It's getting weaker every year. So, yes, that's the plan—to repair the wharf and try to save it for the future.

THE NEXT GENERATION

Gael Watson

I think both my children have their eye on the precarious place the planet is in right now. It's not impossible to turn things around, but it's going to require really hard work, as always. It's going to require a lot of perseverance. Jesse has a really good view of the building itself. His particular quality is that he understands the building and the space in it. He has a really good view of what needs to be done in order to secure it as a very old wooden structure sitting on the edge of the shoreline. Sadie has the skills from her working life in public health. I feel that she is going to make use of the building for more than food; for mental health as well. Thankfully, both Jesse and Sadie have been allowing me to free-range, as long as I'm at the helm. I never feel that they're thinking, "Oh, this is something that Gael should not do." I always feel that they're behind me, and in it. Perhaps, as I grow older, they will move forward. They have not involved themselves with the day-to-day running of the bakery. But they've always contributed to the ideas that move it forward; they keep it moving forward.

All along, Jesse has been involved with the building—since he was very young. Often, I will look to him for his spatial abilities. What would look right; the things that would make something work better, space-wise, in the building. The gallery space, the publisher's office, the grocery store downstairs, my office—all those things have had Jesse's input.

Sadie is just such a steady and capable person. I think she was born that way. It's certainly the way she has been, from such a young age, that enabled me to really pay attention to how things were going at the bakery. I was so busy, and Sadie just had this knowledge of how things work in the building. She's a

Sadie Watson and Jesse Watson at the front door of the LaHave Bakery, c. 2001. (JANE MORRIGAN)

complete natural. As young as she was, I think she picked up on the thing that people feel about the building itself and the energy that it has.

THE GRANDCHILDREN

Gael Watson

When Eamon [Gael's grandson] was five, I was picking him up after school and bringing him to the bakery. He'd help us with various things, like slicing onions with our big food processor. He was into it. Also, on Wednesday, which is payday, he would say, "I do the payroll!" What that meant was, we'd put the paycheques in the envelopes, and Eamon would sticker each one and take them downstairs to the drawer where people go to collect their paycheques. So that was his job that year. He was very interested in mechanical things, like

Gael Watson and grandson, Eamon John Campbell Thompson, seated in the lunchroom of the LaHave Bakery, December 2012. (JANE MORRIGAN)

turning on the fans and turning them off, when he was only a year and a half. I remember, he would've been maybe two, Anna Bald showing him how to make espresso coffee.

Around the time that Eamon was starting to be involved in some things, Covid came along. So Enid [Gael's granddaughter] wasn't here the same way Eamon was when she was little because of that. They haven't been able to be social inside the bakery. When we see each other, it's usually outside of the bakery or at home. They are both very familiar with the building and know where everything is. They know the birds in the back; they'll go and visit them.

Gael Watson with granddaughter, Enid Maria Campbell Watson, coming up the stairs from the Fair Banks Grocery, c. 2021. (JANE MORRIGAN)

Sadie Watson

We were camping at Keji [Kejimkujik National Park] this summer and, quite by accident, I met Jeff McMahon's son and his daughter-in-law and his grandchildren. Jeff grows the wheat for the bakery. In two seconds, we went from, they were admiring the Boler camper, and I was like, "You're from that community? That's where my mum's wheat is grown."

And she's like, "LaHave Bakery?"

And I'm like, "Yeah!"

Nova Scotia. Two seconds; two degrees of separation. We were laughing and saying, "I guess we should get the grandchildren to know each other, because, really, they're the ones—the next generation—who'll be communicating on business."

TRUST

Gael Watson

As you grow older, you're more under scrutiny, and I hope that the scrutiny of the younger people doesn't undo me. I'm trying to move into the future in new ways and with new language. But part of me is steadfast in thinking about what works and what doesn't work; what's healthy and what isn't. I can never really take on a fresh new idea unless there's evidence that it might work. My nature is to stick close to the land, hands on the earth. That may become a thing of the past. Sometimes it's unnerving if an idea is based on a notion of what it is, rather than an understanding of what it is.

My hope is that the bakery will continue; that it will continue to be a source of local food. It's a wonderful processing plant. We can do things on a small scale. Therefore, we are always encouraging people in the area who have gardens to grow specific things—things that we can then transform so they can last through the winter and into the next season. I want to encourage more and more of that.

About twelve years ago, I turned the building into a trust. That meant, for me, my trust was in the future of continuing the building so that my family would have the option to keep it if they wanted to keep it. It's taken a long time—every single year of thirty-six years that I've been here. It takes a long time to do something that is meaningful to a community. There isn't any one thing that's been done here that's made it work. It's a combination of so many ideas.

In the future, it's going to be in the hands of my children, Jesse and Sadie. I'm feeling that they'll take the ball and run, and they'll have their own ideas and their own ways of doing things. Even now, I'm pretty confident that their approach will be similar—that it's for the land and it's for the people who live here. Hopefully, the building will last far into the future.

RETIREMENT

Gael Watson

No, never "retire." I see myself as a ninety-two-year-old, perhaps with a cane, hopefully not too wrinkled up, but still participating in how things go at the bakery—because I question so many things and I wouldn't want to *not* be there to question, and to hear an answer.

But I'm fully prepared to step back. Laura, who is the manager at the moment, is so capable, smart, and able to do so many things. It really depends on the people who are taking part in the bakery. Right now, I'm really comfortable with everybody who's participating. So I may retire, eventually. It's hard to say. I'm sixty-eight now. Ten years is gone in a flash. Twenty years is gone in a flash. If I put ten and twenty years on sixty-eight, that's definitely getting into old age.

A BEACON

Jesse Watson

I've been spending a lot of time lately thinking about the top floor of the building and Homegrown Skateboards—something I haven't spent time thinking about for decades because I was just so "in it." I recognize that I can't continue to steamroll through and carry the weight of this space physically the way I did, particularly about skateboarding. I am increasingly more comfortable with that. I want to be fluid with how the space represents what I have so much passion for, and how it has made Homegrown go from the early '90s to now. I don't want to lose the momentum of what the space has been for so many generations of people who've been involved with it—a place for creative expression.

My mandate or mission statement for the top floor—in legitimately honouring the work and the opportunity I've been given—also carries through to the rest of the building and the bakery. That would be this: that the entire building continues to reflect the importance of quality food, the people who work here, and the people of all ages who are welcome here. And that it can be a beacon in a rural area.

Things are always changing and moving. How difficult it must be for Gael and everyone downstairs to continue to provide real food, not just to wealthy people, but to everyone. And I'm sure that challenge isn't going to go away soon. Whatever my level of responsibility becomes downstairs in the building, it will always be connected to quality food available to regular people.

IN THE WINGS

Sadie Watson

When I think about coming back to the bakery and getting involved in the business, it feels pretty terrifying, if I'm honest. I'm a little apprehensive, because it's a real shifting of gears. I have established a completely separate career. In a way, it's turning back to what was. I keep going back to this analogy: what was colourful, what smelled good, what brought a lot of new people and new ideas into my life. That was my foundation. That was my upbringing, and so I am excited about returning to that environment, which is this place. Nervous about any skills that I've lost. I've been working with policy, health promotion, Covid emergency relief—a very different world. It will be a bizarre and sharp pivot into this realm again, which has changed a lot. All new people, pretty much, since I was last involved fifteen years ago. I don't know what people's expectations are; reservations. That's in the back of my head. Will I be able to meet expectations when I don't even know what the expectations are?

There's also this incredible excitement about the opportunities, both with the building and with the business. They're so limitless, and Gael has demonstrated that. With the grocery store, I was, "You know, this would be really interesting," and then the next week she's knocking down walls. And I was, like, "Okay..."

The world that I've been working in, in government, I've been trying to knock down walls. It's not impossible. But it is really hard to protect your own values and beliefs and to have vision and push at the same time. The wheels of government turn slowly, and that's the world I've been in. Whereas at the bakery, the wheels turn really quickly. I'm trying to anticipate what coming back into this world will feel like. I've grown quite methodical and organized in the way that I do my work. At the bakery, Gael sometimes just needs to mutate, survive, reinvent, cut here, go there. It's a different way than I've been working. I'm trying to get my head around getting ready to work and live and think differently. I'm hoping that the two of us, with Laura, will come together and merge all of those skill sets, that it will be beneficial for us personally, and also for the business.

I'm going back to the opportunities and there's tons—both to support what's happening now and also, potentially, to look to the water again. Look at the opportunities of welcoming international travelers again. I miss that. When Bruce and I came back to live on the South Shore in Nova Scotia, I intended to come and go; to travel. With Covid, for the last two years, I have stayed in one place. It has given me this great craving for connection. Now, with our sensitivity about travel, we are able to look at more sustainable, low-impact ways of welcoming people and sharing this community. Rethinking. Travelling on a boat is lower-impact than flying. How can we begin to promote the Port of LaHave again? A lot of that was Mike's, my dad's, vision. That was on point, and I would love to explore and get back to that. Gael is continuing to maintain that. You add another person and you might have a little bit more energy to cover another base. It's hard to cover all bases, so hopefully we'll be able to support each other, having a more even distribution of how we invest energy and what that would look like.

Hopefully, I will bring something to the business. I've been a project manager, an acting director, an innovator, an advocate. I've been a writer and a researcher. I've had to employ a lot of diplomacy in my work, always with a lens on equity, on understanding people's social and emotional and mental health. Also, in terms of income, what does it mean if individuals don't have sustainable income? What does it mean if people don't have sustainable housing? Those who don't have sustainable income and housing are generally the people who feed us; who feed the population. Gael and Laura already have a lens on this. I'm hoping that what I can bring is how do we do this better. How do we support people who work in the space and for the business?

Inside LaHave River Books looking out over the wharf toward the sea, 2017. (Jim Bell)

Fair Banks Grocery, 2023. (Jim Bell)

ABOVE: *Gael Watson ascending the stairs from the bread kitchen, c. 2021.* (Jane Morrigan)

FACING PAGE: *The LaHave Bakery staff on Hawaiian Day. From top left: Shelley Tracey, Darby Van Tassel, Barb Smith; bottom row from left: Brenda-gail Toth, Anna Bald, Joanne Risser, c. 2002.* (Unknown)

Laura Pitts at the LaHave Bakery shop counter, 2012. (Jim Bell)

LaHave Bakery customers entering and relaxing in front of the Outfitters building, c. 2017. (Jane Morrigan)

Activity at the LaHave Bakery wharf and floating dock, c. 1998. (Unknown)

The LaHave Bakery lunchroom during Covid, c. 2021; this room was formerly the accounting office for the LaHave Outfitting Company. (Jane Morrigan)

ABOVE: *This intricate painting by Anna Bald provides a peek into the interior of the LaHave Outfitters building, 2023.* (ANNA BALD)

BELOW: *A watercolour painting by Leslie Snidal of the LaHave Bakery, c. 2015.* (LESLIE SNIDAL)

Now you can make the LaHave Bakery breads yourself! Find the recipes here:

1. Anadama Bread, page 202
2. Cheddar Cheese and Herb Bread, page 204
3. Milk and Honey Bread, page 206
4. Oatmeal Molasses Honey Bread, page 208
5. Potato Bread, page 210
6. Raisin Orange Bread, page 212
7. Seed Bread, page 214

Find the recipes for all of these sweets on the following pages:

1. Butter Tarts, page 220
2. Carrot Cake, page 222
3. Date Squares, page 224
4. Lemon Squares, page 226
5. Mocha Cake, page 228

So I think I can bring those things, as well as hustle. That's my speed. Hopefully, just by hustling, it will be helpful—extra hands on deck. I hope that Gael will be able to find a way to step back. Not a lot, but a little, if she wants to work less. This will hopefully be an opportunity for balance—for all three of us to be able to have a higher quality of life, and also for Gael to be able to feel that it's okay to disengage mentally for a day or two.

We'll see. We really need to test it. Maybe it's not going to work. I don't know, but I'm stepping away a little from the world that I've been in, in the hopes that we can trial it and that it will work—that it will work for all of us.

CHAPTER 17

Reflections

PERSPECTIVE

Gael Watson

I do it because it's fun, it's worthwhile, it's meaningful. I do it because, from an early age, I always appreciated what has gone before, the efforts and the energy that it took to reach any point. That continues for me, that appreciation. If you look back and really examine the adversities of people who first came here, the tools they had, and the time they took. The perseverance. Everyone who's on board is always starting on a point that has been left by previous generations. I feel that I'm just part of that fabric—part of the fabric and the pattern and the design. At the same time, I am also part of the designing and part of the weave. I have choices I can make to expand on things that strike me as being important. But I'm only a piece of it, and so was the person before me and the generations before me. They were pieces.

You just have to keep your eye on the ball. If you see that a direction is a positive thing, and you see in your own life that you've been able to create change—maybe small but positive change—then I'm in it. I can see that. I might get tired, but I've certainly never backed away from feeling strongly that I can be a part of what can make change; good change. It's all interpretation: "What I say is good." But the benefit of staying in one place long enough is that you see the people are happy that the building is there. I don't feel that people think, "What a waste. What a waste of time and energy, saving that building."

Saving the building has been a part of saving something that is worthwhile, and looking into the future—looking into the future, and building on it.

This comes from an appreciation that we had as children for a piece of handmade furniture or a pasture that had been kept up. Old roads through the woods. I think it begins with learning about the past and having an intimate involvement with the past. The closer you can get to understanding the way things were, the more you can appreciate it and identify with it as a modern person. For me, following an old recipe from the war, from the Second World War, gives me an appreciation of what was in it, what was available to use for food, and innovative ideas that came out of that lack of variety. Travel to stay with our Jamaican friends gave me a view into how you could be healthy with way less. So to desire more in terms of more equipment, more technology, can be a tool, but it can also strip you of the knowledge of what we need most: clean air, clean water, and clean land from which we can grow food. Those are the basics. It helps to look back, into the past, to see that so many generations either thrived or died, depending on whether they had those things.

When I sit down at night, I think about the millions of people who are living a life that has so little. It motivates me to always be thinking that there must be a better way. Surely there is. If you steer your mind towards something that you perceive is better, a lot of the time you can edge forward a little bit. I'm always conscious of the rest of the world. I'm always conscious of all the animals in the middle of the night, on a cold night—thinking of the animals that are outside. When there is a heat wave or a drought, when there is famine or disease. It's hard to separate yourself from that. So even though I'm living the life and I have a warm, comfortable house, and I have enough wood to burn through the winter, and I have more food than I need to eat, I'm never not thinking of everybody else on the planet—"Are they all right tonight?" And they are not. And knowing that they're not, a lot of them are not, then it keeps you feeling serious about the value of your own life and the shortness of it. Whether or not you can contribute in a positive way, it is very motivating to be aware of the rest of the world, the rest of the animals, the rest of the forest, and the ocean itself.

I can't imagine doing it differently. I would have to be a different person. All the players would have to be different; all the situations; my entire upbringing; everything would have to be different. I did the best I could with what I am and what I've learned, and what I was capable of learning. So I can't imagine doing anything differently. I can imagine that I wish things hadn't gone the way they did sometimes. But I think you can't be happy unless you've been sad. You can't; you have to be able to cry. If you can't cry, if you can't weep, if you can't know losses, then you can't see the other side.

There's never been a time that I've thought I should give it up. I've never been in a quitting mood. The experience of the bakery—I'm just one of the lucky ones.

SUPPORT

Gael Watson

What has made it possible? I would say encouragement and support from my family, my friends, and my children. I have been helped by my family; my friends have stood by me; customers who were sympathetic; animals who were there. I've been helped a lot. I didn't do it on my own. Realizing it is a gift that I've been able to do this—that it's worked out this way.

Peggy always said, "You can do this and it's going to work." She said it with such confidence that it really had an impact on me, because Peggy's really smart, like Marion. My two friends were very smart people, so it really mattered that Peggy was saying this. I'll always remember that, because there were other people who were shaking their heads and saying, "You have no idea what you're getting into." "You can't do that." "You're not going to be able to do it; you'll find out." And Peggy was not that way. It was very wonderful that Peggy and Marion were there for me.

Kathy Fisher became a real godsend for me. She became my friend—really monumental in my life—somebody who was looking out for me. She was smart and sharp. It felt more like a partnership, even though she worked for and was paid by the bakery. She worked with me in the office, too, as the manager. Right to the end. I miss her; a good person who succumbed. She worked on a Monday and died on a Wednesday. When I went to the Fishermen's Memorial Hospital in Lunenburg because the time had come, unbelievably, I kneeled down beside her. I remember looking at her and both of us whispering, "Go figure." She wanted to live. I wanted her to live. She tried so hard. She

Gael Watson's stalwart friends. From left, the late Marion Garlick, Gael Watson, and Peggy Greer in Gael's overgrown garden, Crousetown, c. 1999. (UNKNOWN)

Gael Watson and Kathy (Wamback) Fisher taking a break on the steps to the third-floor apartment and hostel, c. 1992. (UNKNOWN)

did everything she could, and it didn't stop her from dying. And that was a chapter, her death.

COMMUNITY

Sadie Watson

Initially, there was probably a lot of eyebrow-raising. Mike and Gael bought the building, and at that point the back of it was falling into the river. So I think it was, "Pfff, what are these kids up to?" I'm guessing there was skepticism that they would actually be able to make a go of it. And they did. They pulled the building out of the river. That was Mike's early work. It was instrumental in this building's survival. Then Gael, establishing the bakery—hustling, not giving up, providing employment, finding the way to make it work when it was really financially extremely difficult to stay afloat. The bakery has stayed for my entire life, from when I was a year old to now; I'm thirty-eight now.

I think that the bakery has demonstrated resilience, but it also has held fast LaHave's sustained hub. How to describe it? LaHave has always been a hub, but I think the bakery and the building has supported a bit of a revival in the community. I remember running into David Himmelman, maybe when I was in high school with his kids, and he was like, "Yup, bread and fish. That's what LaHave is all about." And it really was, for a long time—there was bread and fish. The smells were bread and fish when the boats came in, because fish is his business.

I always thought that that was really interesting to be way out here at the estuary of the LaHave River and to continue to contribute to this community—not just be a cluster of houses that you drive through. It's a village and a centre point. And it's not just the bakery. It all pulls together. You've got the ferry, the fish plant, the bakery. Now there's a pottery shop. Now there's a jewellery shop. There's a whole bunch of different amazing artists along the stretch. But I think that the bakery has been part of that living organism.

I want to be really careful because a lot of people worked really hard to establish themselves in LaHave, and not because of the bakery. But I think it is a contributing factor to why the village is what it is today. There was Murray Farr and Gloria Barrett and the people who were here before, in terms of "come-from-aways." They were sort of the early artistic inspiration. Mike and

Gael were able to dig in and have the vision, and you see there have been many waves since—people who were inspired and moved here. Musicians, for example, in the area. They then bring others. And I think the bakery has done that: it's brought others who are inspired in a similar way. As for the local community, I'm not sure how they felt about two people coming in from away, but when I was a kid, everyone was welcoming. At least that's my experience—that people were patient and welcoming. Even if the bread wasn't exactly what they would normally buy, they were still coming to buy the milk. There are still neighbours that I see who have never bought the bread, but they still come in for milk and butter.

GIFTS

Gael Watson

The bakery has given me a lot of pleasure. The people I've met who came through the doors—the customers and the ones who worked at the bakery. It's always been like an art form to me. It's given me a palette. It's just unlimited—places where you can be creative and imagine.

It's been a great gift to me, as it's turned out. Who would've thought that it would last, in the beginning? Nobody. I had no idea; no idea. I certainly didn't think it would fail, but I just didn't think that far. There was just always something to do, always something to improve, always a project. The building was so big that it offered so many possibilities. Not that I knew what those possibilities were, but I just rolled with the bakery. Adversity—as it turns out, I work well with adversity and have always been able to think more clearly under unexpected or uncomfortable or dire situations. I learned that about myself. Now that the building has come so far, is stronger and is fixed up, things are easier for me. I have the wonderful advantage of still having it, and knowing that all that work, all the strife, all the ups and the downs, the catastrophes, didn't end it. Breaking through to the other side, eventually; reaching the point where the debt was paid off. You're out of prison. The freedom! The level of anxiety diminishes hugely when you don't have debt. You can start doing things for fun, not just the basics of putting in new sills; those things are always going to happen with an old building. That's the gift—being able to still be here, growing and moving through the times, and not being flattened by it. The feeling that the community of LaHave is happy that the bakery is here. Except maybe not with the traffic in the summer! I overhear conversations and I'm really happy that it's not just me who's loving the building.

What am I most proud of? That we make darn good food here. I'm proud that we can do that. But there isn't one day that you're not on that thin wedge. You can never know for sure how long things will last or if that one wrong move is going take it away from you. It's always there, crisis—it's always around the corner. But when you're not in crisis, you're able to breathe and appreciate everything that you have—everything that surrounds you, the air that you breathe, the place where you live, the security of having a meal on the table, the beauty of what you drive through in the morning. When you look out and it's peaceful, even if it's only for ten minutes, I can just accept when it's right for that moment and take it in, breathe it in, hold it in, and know that it's going to see me through the next crisis. That is something that has been given to me because of the bakery.

Peggy Greer

It's been a joy to have watched this wild and strange journey. It's been fun to have been a bit player in it and wonderful to have been Gael's buddy through it all. But I will say it wasn't easy; it wasn't easy at all. The Gael I know is a very shy, private person, and for her to become a public person has been, in itself, a great challenge. So that has been part of the journey too, and has been interesting to watch.

LEGACY

Peggy Greer

It's a long time; thirty-six years. It's a long time to maintain a business—to push it up the hill and sometimes just have it chase you back down again. It's been challenging for Gael. The entire community is grateful for what she has done and for what she is still doing. She has trained young people and they have gone out into the world. Some have come back. She has shown all of them that their dreams are possible, which is pretty big stuff! That's a huge thing in my mind—to present possibilities for how dreams can become true. That's the best that can happen, really. The ultimate gift. That's what she has given to the community.

In some ways, what she has created has been responsible for drawing brilliant young people to this area. They settle. They have children. It's brought life to a dying community, to the whole area. That's big stuff; that's worth noting.

Laura Pitts

In the time that I've known Gael, she's run the business as a solitary person. Gael is very independent, and I think it's really inspiring to a lot of young women—women my age. They feel like it's not out of the realm to buy this and fix it up. "I'm going to build my own house," or "I'm going to live by myself," or "I'm going to have a child on my own," or "I'm going to do all this stuff." I think that Gael does have an influence on decisions that people have made.

Andra White

And now look at where Gael is. Yeah—who would have known? But she stuck with it. She downplayed how much she did, but she just stuck with it and made the place what it is today. She really was a mentor for many of these people that came along after, and she was so supportive of them, to help them along the way. Always giving great advice.

Peggy Greer

She had a dream, created the dream, and that dream allowed others to dream and create their own dreams. I think that's her legacy.

The Baker

A poem by Gael Watson

LaHave, c. 1991

In the cavern of the building
the nocturnal baker is working,
music keeping her company.
Sometimes she dances,
sometimes she weeps.
No one will know—
only the bread
in the dead of night.

Most people are sleeping;
the air is filled with their dreams—
alive and fluid.
Edging towards her mute state,
hands work deftly.
Her mind comes and goes,
returning with the voices of the dawn.

Part 5

The Recipes

CHAPTER 18

A Taste of LaHave Bakery:
A Baker's Dozen

Gael Watson

MY LOVE OF BAKING COMES FROM MY GRANDMOTHER, EFFIE DAVIDSON, MY PARents, Donald and Enid Robertson, and my aunt, Rhoda Davidson. All the adults who raised us. They liked to bake, and they made different things. My father with his cheese scones, cheese straws, and onion bread. My mother made brownies and date squares, muffins and butter tarts, and lots of cookies. She was always baking things for us to find after school. My aunt made a delicious lemon poppy seed cake. My grandmother, with her tea biscuits and her baking skills. My mother would say my grandmother never followed a recipe. She knew how to put things together; she knew the chemistry of it, which always impressed me. That family association with baking has been very comforting to me. It's what got me started.

I love cookbooks! One of my favourite books is a cookbook that my sister Jane gave me. An ancient cookbook, printed in England in 1719—at this point, over three hundred years old. It's very "olde English" with Fs as Ss and their Ss as Fs. Most of the book has recipes in it, but it also has cures; cures for things like "The King's Evil," where the King would kiss you to cure you, and "Convulsions." They were sort of like witchcraft. It's a fascinating book. Wonderful books through history tell you so many things about how people were living, and what was available to them. Some of the herbs that were used are still very common. Other ones I've never heard of before, but they were commonly grown in peoples' backyards because that was what they relied on for their health and to cure all manner of illnesses.

In the early years of the bakery, this old book was really precious to me, especially when things were overwhelming. I would sit down with a cup of tea and take that book in my hands, and I'd turn the pages. Just the thought that someone, three hundred years ago, had read that book, had followed the recipes, and had lived a life. For some reason I found that very consoling.

Bread Recipes

(Jim Bell)

HELPFUL BREAD-MAKING TIPS

- Never add salt to the yeast while it is activating. Salt will inhibit the yeast at that stage. On the other hand, salt strengthens the gluten when added later in the bread-making process.

- Begin mixing bread dough by hand with a wooden spoon, gradually adding the flour. As you do so, the dough will become stiffer and more difficult to beat. Do this until you can't beat by hand any longer; the more exertion you put into this stage, the less time it will take to knead the dough. (By beating and kneading, you are developing the gluten strands, which are becoming strong and encapsulating the carbon dioxide gas, which gives the bread the ability to rise and lighten.)

- During the first rise, the time required for the dough to double in size varies depending on how warm or cool your kitchen is. A warm rise takes roughly two hours; a cool rise takes longer, but the bread is often tastier that way.

- These recipes describe the process for making two round loaves. If you want to make two rectangular loaves, simply place each half of the dough into a well-oiled standard loaf pan before the second rise. The baking time will be the same.

- During the second rise, the dough needs to double in size again, but do not allow it to rise to more than double in size, because the yeast will begin to consume the sugars, causing it to weaken—and possibly deflating the bread.

Anadama

MAKES 2 ROUND LOAVES

- 1 cup plus 2 tablespoons lukewarm water (80 to 85°F), divided
- 1 teaspoon honey
- 1 tablespoon traditional dry yeast
- 2 cups boiling water
- ½ cup cornmeal
- ¼ cup butter, melted
- 1 teaspoon sea salt
- ½ cup molasses
- 1 tablespoon plus 2 teaspoons oil, divided
- 2 beaten eggs, divided
- 1 cup stone-ground whole wheat flour
- 5 cups unbleached white wheat flour, separated

(Jim Bell)

NOTE: PLEASE READ HELPFUL TIPS ON P. 201 BEFORE BEGINNING.

In a small bowl, stir together ½ cup of the lukewarm water and the honey. Sprinkle the yeast on top. Do not stir. Set mixture aside for 5 to 10 minutes to activate yeast.

In a large bowl, stir together the boiling water, cornmeal, butter, and salt. Allow to cool just a little, then stir in molasses, ½ cup of the lukewarm water, 2 teaspoons of the oil, and 1 beaten egg. While mixture is warm, stir in the softened yeast mixture.

Add whole wheat flour and 2 cups of the white flour. With a wooden spoon, beat energetically, until the gluten is developing well and pulling together. Continue to add more flour, 1 cup at a time, until you can't stir any longer.

When you find the dough too difficult to mix with the spoon, turn it out onto a lightly floured surface and knead in remaining flour, adding only enough flour to keep the dough from sticking to your hands, until you have a pliable consistency—not too sticky, not too dry. Knead gently and rhythmically, but with strength, until the dough is smooth and elastic.

Clean the large bowl and oil with 1 tablespoon of the vegetable oil. Return the dough to the bowl, turning dough to coat the surface. Cover bowl with a tea towel and place in a warm spot, allowing the dough to rise until doubled in size—roughly 2 hours or longer, depending on how warm your kitchen is.

When the dough has risen, gently press out the carbon dioxide with your fist and fold the dough over itself, turning it out onto a lightly floured counter. Divide into two even pieces. Knead each gently—a few strokes to free air pockets and bubbles—and shape into two round loaves. Lightly grease a cookie sheet with vegetable oil. Place loaves well apart on prepared cookie sheet.

Beat remaining egg into the remaining 2 tablespoons of the lukewarm water and glaze each loaf with this egg wash.

Cover with a tea towel and allow to rise again until just doubled in size—generally about half the time of the first rise.

Preheat oven to 400°F.

Bake for 15 minutes, then reduce oven temperature to 375°F and bake for about 35 minutes. Bread is done when the bottom sounds hollow when tapped.

Cool on a wire rack or wooden breadboard.

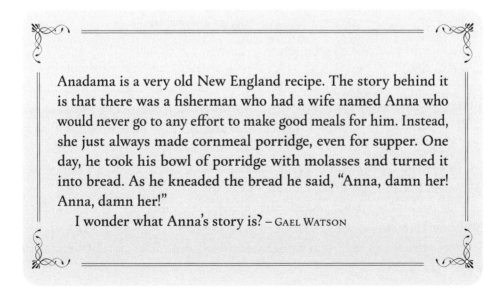

Anadama is a very old New England recipe. The story behind it is that there was a fisherman who had a wife named Anna who would never go to any effort to make good meals for him. Instead, she just always made cornmeal porridge, even for supper. One day, he took his bowl of porridge with molasses and turned it into bread. As he kneaded the bread he said, "Anna, damn her! Anna, damn her!"

I wonder what Anna's story is? – GAEL WATSON

Cheddar Cheese & Herb

MAKES 2 ROUND LOAVES

- 2½ cups plus 2 tablespoons lukewarm water (80 to 85°F), divided
- 1 teaspoon honey
- 1 tablespoon traditional dry yeast
- 1 onion, roughly chopped
- 2 cloves garlic, roughly chopped
- 1 teaspoon dried oregano
- 1 teaspoon dried basil
- ½ teaspoon dried rosemary
- 1 tablespoon sea salt
- 2 eggs
- 4 tablespoons vegetable oil, divided
- 5 to 6 cups unbleached white wheat flour
- 1 cup grated cheddar cheese

(JIM BELL)

NOTE: PLEASE READ HELPFUL TIPS ON P. 201 BEFORE BEGINNING.

In a small bowl, stir together ½ cup of the lukewarm water and the honey. Sprinkle the yeast over the surface. Do not stir. Set mixture aside for 5 to 10 minutes to activate yeast.

In a blender, place onion, garlic, oregano, basil, rosemary, salt, 2 cups of the lukewarm water, 1 egg, and 3 tablespoons of the oil. Blend.

Pour into a large bowl and add the softened yeast mixture. Stir to combine. Add flour, 1 cup at a time, beating with a wooden spoon until the gluten is developing well and pulling together. Continue to add flour until you can't stir any longer.

When you find the dough too difficult to mix with the spoon, turn it out onto a lightly floured surface and knead in remaining flour, adding only enough flour to keep the dough from sticking to your hands, until you have a pliable consistency—not too sticky, not too dry. Knead gently and rhythmically, but with strength, until the dough is smooth and elastic.

Clean the large bowl and oil with 1 tablespoon of the vegetable oil. Return the dough to the bowl, turning the dough to coat the surface. Cover bowl with a tea towel and place in a warm spot, allowing the dough to rise until doubled in size—roughly 2 hours or longer, depending on how warm your kitchen is.

When the dough has risen, gently press out the carbon dioxide with your fist and fold the dough over itself, turning it out onto a lightly floured counter. Divide into two even pieces. Knead each gently—a few strokes to free air pockets and bubbles—and shape into two round loaves. Lightly grease a cookie sheet with vegetable oil. Place loaves well apart on prepared cookie sheet.

Slash the tops diagonally several times. Beat 1 egg into the remaining 2 tablespoons of the lukewarm water and glaze loaves with this egg wash. Sprinkle with grated cheddar cheese.

Cover with a tea towel and allow to rise again until just doubled in size—generally about half the time of the first rise.

Preheat oven to 375°F.

Bake for 40 to 50 minutes. You will know that the loaves are fully baked when they are a beautiful golden colour and sound hollow when tapped on the bottom.

Cool on a wire rack or wooden breadboard.

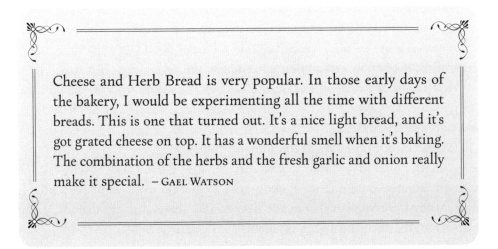

> Cheese and Herb Bread is very popular. In those early days of the bakery, I would be experimenting all the time with different breads. This is one that turned out. It's a nice light bread, and it's got grated cheese on top. It has a wonderful smell when it's baking. The combination of the herbs and the fresh garlic and onion really make it special. – GAEL WATSON

Milk & Honey

MAKES 2 ROUND LOAVES

- 1/3 cup plus 1 teaspoon honey, divided
- 1½ cups plus 2 tablespoons lukewarm water (80 to 85°F), divided
- 1 tablespoon traditional dry yeast
- 3 tablespoons canola oil or melted butter
- 1 cup whole milk, warm
- 1 tablespoon sea salt
- 3 beaten eggs, divided
- 5 to 6 cups unbleached white wheat flour

(JIM BELL)

NOTE: PLEASE READ HELPFUL TIPS ON P. 201 BEFORE BEGINNING.

In a large bowl, stir together 1 teaspoon of the honey and ½ cup of the lukewarm water. Sprinkle in the yeast. Do not stir. Set mixture aside for 5 to 10 minutes to activate yeast.

After resting this mixture, add 2 tablespoons of the oil, 1/3 cup of the honey, 1 cup of the lukewarm water, milk, salt, and 2 of the beaten eggs. Stir to combine.

Add 3 cups of the flour and commence beating with a wooden spoon until the gluten is developing well and pulling together. Continue to add flour until you can't stir any longer.

When you find the dough too difficult to mix with the spoon, turn it out onto a lightly floured surface and knead in remaining flour, adding only enough flour to keep the dough from sticking to your hands, until you have a pliable consistency—not too sticky, not too dry. Knead gently and rhythmically, but with strength, until the dough is smooth and elastic.

Clean the large bowl and oil with 1 tablespoon of the oil. Return the dough to the bowl, turning the dough to coat the surface. Cover bowl with a tea towel and place in a warm spot, allowing the dough to rise until doubled in size—roughly 2 hours or longer, depending on how warm your kitchen is.

When the dough has risen, gently press out the carbon dioxide with your fist and fold the dough over itself, turning it out onto a lightly floured counter. Divide into two even pieces. Knead each gently—a few strokes to free air pockets and bubbles—and shape into two round loaves. Lightly grease a cookie sheet with vegetable oil. Place loaves well apart on prepared cookie sheet.

Slash the tops diagonally several times with a sharp knife. Beat the remaining egg into the remaining 2 tablespoons of the lukewarm water and glaze both loaves with this egg wash.

Cover with a tea towel and allow to rise again until just doubled in size—generally about half the time of the first rise.

Preheat oven to 400°F. Bake for 40 to 50 minutes, until each loaf is a beautiful golden colour and sounds hollow when tapped on the bottom.

Cool on a wire rack or wooden breadboard.

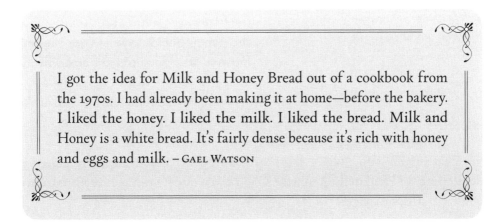

I got the idea for Milk and Honey Bread out of a cookbook from the 1970s. I had already been making it at home—before the bakery. I liked the honey. I liked the milk. I liked the bread. Milk and Honey is a white bread. It's fairly dense because it's rich with honey and eggs and milk. – GAEL WATSON

Oatmeal Molasses Honey

MAKES 2 ROUND LOAVES

- ½ cup plus 2 tablespoons lukewarm water (80 to 85°F), divided
- ¼ cup plus 1 teaspoon honey, divided
- 1 tablespoon traditional dry yeast
- 1½ cup regular rolled oats, divided
- 1 tablespoon sea salt
- ½ cup molasses
- 3 tablespoons melted butter
- 2 cups boiling water
- 3 beaten eggs, divided
- 2 cups stone-ground whole wheat flour
- 4 cups unbleached white wheat flour
- 1 tablespoon vegetable oil

(JIM BELL)

NOTE: PLEASE READ HELPFUL TIPS ON P. 201 BEFORE BEGINNING.

In a small bowl, stir together ½ cup of the lukewarm water and 1 teaspoon of the honey. Sprinkle yeast over the top. Do not stir. Set mixture aside for at least 5 to 10 minutes to activate yeast.

In a large bowl, combine 1 cup of the rolled oats, the remaining ¼ cup of the honey, the salt, molasses, butter, and boiling water. Allow to cool to lukewarm. Stir in 2 of the beaten eggs. Stir in the softened yeast mixture.

Beat in the whole wheat flour with a wooden spoon until the gluten is developing well and pulling together. Add the white flour, 1 cup at a time, until you can't stir any longer.

When you find the dough too difficult to mix with the spoon, turn it out onto a lightly floured surface and knead in remaining flour, adding only enough flour to keep the dough from sticking to your hands, until you have a pliable consistency—not too sticky, not too dry. Knead gently and rhythmically, but with strength, until the dough is smooth and elastic.

Clean the large bowl and oil with the vegetable oil. Return the dough to the bowl, turning the dough to coat the surface. Cover bowl with a tea towel and place in a warm spot, allowing the dough to rise until doubled in size—roughly 2 hours or longer, depending on how warm your kitchen is.

When the dough has risen, gently press out the carbon dioxide with your fist and fold the dough over itself, turning it out onto a lightly floured counter. Divide into two even pieces. Knead each gently—a few strokes to free air pockets and bubbles—and shape into two round loaves. Lightly grease a cookie sheet with vegetable oil.

Roll the loaves in the remaining ½ cup of rolled oats to cover the surface of each and place well apart on prepared cookie sheet.

Beat remaining egg into the remaining 2 tablespoons of the lukewarm water and glaze loaves with this egg wash to hold the oats in place.

Cover with a tea towel and allow to rise again until just doubled in size—generally about half the time of the first rise.

Preheat oven to 400°F. Bake for 15 minutes, then reduce oven temperature to 375°F and continue to bake for about 35 minutes, or until loaves sound hollow when tapped on the bottom. (Check occasionally throughout this time; if top is browning too much, cover lightly with foil.)

Cool on a wire rack or wooden breadboard.

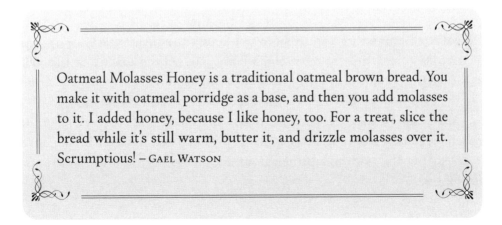

Oatmeal Molasses Honey is a traditional oatmeal brown bread. You make it with oatmeal porridge as a base, and then you add molasses to it. I added honey, because I like honey, too. For a treat, slice the bread while it's still warm, butter it, and drizzle molasses over it. Scrumptious! – GAEL WATSON

Potato Bread

MAKES 2 ROUND LOAVES

- ½ cup plus 2 tablespoons lukewarm water (80 to 85°F), divided
- 2 tablespoons plus 1 teaspoon honey, divided
- 1 tablespoon traditional dry yeast
- 3 tablespoons vegetable oil, divided
- 1½ cups reserved cooking water from the potatoes, warm
- 1 tablespoon sea salt
- 3 beaten eggs, divided
- 1 cup cooked and mashed potatoes
- 5½ cups unbleached white wheat flour
- 2 tablespoons sesame seeds

(JIM BELL)

NOTE: PLEASE READ HELPFUL TIPS ON P. 201 BEFORE BEGINNING.

In a small bowl, mix ½ cup of the lukewarm water and 1 teaspoon of the honey, then sprinkle yeast over the top. Do not stir. Set mixture aside for 5 to 10 minutes to activate yeast.

In a large bowl, mix the remaining 2 tablespoons of the honey, 2 tablespoons of the oil, the potato water (or a mix of warm water and potato water), salt, and 2 of the eggs. Stir in softened yeast mixture. Stir in mashed potatoes.

Add 2 cups of the flour and beat well with a wooden spoon to develop the gluten. Gradually add in the rest of the flour, 1 cup at a time, until the gluten is developing and pulling together. Continue to add flour until you can't stir any longer.

When the dough is too difficult to mix with the spoon, turn it out onto a lightly floured surface and knead in remaining flour, adding only enough flour to keep the dough from sticking to your hands, until you have a pliable consistency—not too sticky, not too dry. Knead gently and rhythmically, but with strength, until the dough is smooth and elastic.

Clean the large bowl and oil with 1 tablespoon of the vegetable oil. Return the dough to the bowl, turning the dough to coat the surface. Cover bowl with a tea towel and place in a warm spot, allowing the dough to rise until doubled in size—roughly 2 hours or longer, depending on how warm your kitchen is.

When the dough has risen, gently press out the carbon dioxide with your fist and fold the dough over itself, turning it out onto a lightly floured counter. Divide into two even pieces. Knead each gently—a few strokes to free air pockets and bubbles—and shape into two round loaves. Lightly grease a cookie sheet with vegetable oil. Place loaves well apart on prepared cookie sheet.

Beat the remaining egg into the remaining 2 tablespoons of the lukewarm water and glaze loaves with this egg wash. Sprinkle sesame seeds over the tops of the loaves.

Cover with a tea towel and allow to rise again until just doubled in size—generally about half the time of the first rise.

Preheat oven to 400°F. Bake 35 to 40 minutes, or until loaves are golden and sound hollow when tapped on the bottom.

Cool on a wire rack or wooden breadboard.

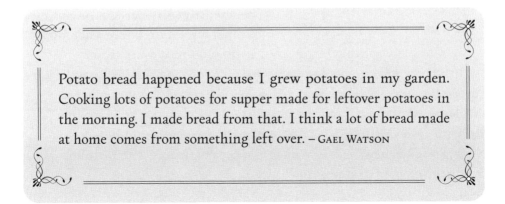

> Potato bread happened because I grew potatoes in my garden. Cooking lots of potatoes for supper made for leftover potatoes in the morning. I made bread from that. I think a lot of bread made at home comes from something left over. – GAEL WATSON

Raisin Orange

MAKES 2 ROUND LOAVES

- 1½ cups raisins
- 1½ cups lukewarm orange juice (80 to 85°F), divided
- 1½ cups plus 2 tablespoons lukewarm water (80 to 85°F), divided
- ⅓ cup plus 1 teaspoon honey, divided
- 1 tablespoon traditional dry yeast
- 2 beaten eggs, divided
- 4 tablespoons plus 1 teaspoon vegetable oil, divided
- 1 teaspoon cinnamon
- 1 teaspoon ginger
- 1 teaspoon nutmeg
- 1 cup whole wheat flour
- 5 cups unbleached white wheat flour

(JIM BELL)

NOTE: PLEASE READ HELPFUL TIPS ON P. 201 BEFORE BEGINNING.

Add raisins to ½ cup of the lukewarm orange juice and soak for 20 minutes.

In a small bowl, mix ½ cup of the lukewarm water and 1 teaspoon of the honey, then sprinkle yeast on mixture. Do not stir. Set mixture aside for 5 to 10 minutes to activate yeast.

In a large bowl, combine remaining 1 cup of the lukewarm orange juice, the remaining 1 cup of the lukewarm water, the remaining ⅓ cup honey, 1 egg, 3 tablespoons of the oil, and the softened raisins along with the soaking juice. Stir with a wooden spoon.

In a medium bowl, mix cinnamon, ginger, and nutmeg with the whole wheat flour. Stir into wet mixture.

To the large bowl, add white flour, 1 cup at a time, beating with a wooden spoon until the gluten is developing well and pulling together. Continue to add flour until you can't stir any longer.

When you find the dough too difficult to mix with the spoon, turn it out onto a lightly floured surface and knead in remaining flour, adding only enough flour to keep the dough from sticking to your hands, until you have a pliable consistency—not too sticky, not too dry. Knead gently and rhythmically, but with strength, until the dough is smooth and elastic.

Clean the large bowl and oil with 1 tablespoon of the vegetable oil. Return the dough to the bowl, turning the dough to coat the surface. Cover bowl with a tea towel and place in a warm spot, allowing the dough to rise until doubled in size—roughly 2 hours or longer, depending on how warm your kitchen is.

When the dough has risen, gently press out the carbon dioxide with your fist and fold the dough over itself, turning it out onto a lightly floured counter. Divide into two even pieces. Knead each gently—a few strokes to free air pockets and bubbles—and shape into two round loaves. Lightly grease a cookie sheet with vegetable oil. Place loaves well apart on prepared cookie sheet.

Beat remaining egg into the remaining 2 tablespoons of lukewarm water and glaze loaves with this egg wash.

Allow to rise again, uncovered, until just doubled in size—generally about half the time of the first rise.

Preheat oven to 400°F. Bake for 15 minutes, then reduce the oven temperature to 375°F and bake about 35 minutes longer or until the bottoms sound hollow when you tap them.

Cool on a wire rack or wooden breadboard.

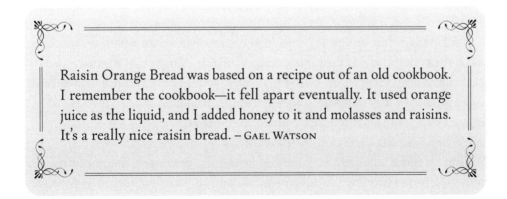

Raisin Orange Bread was based on a recipe out of an old cookbook. I remember the cookbook—it fell apart eventually. It used orange juice as the liquid, and I added honey to it and molasses and raisins. It's a really nice raisin bread. – GAEL WATSON

Seed Bread

MAKES 2 ROUND LOAVES

- 2½ cups plus 2 tablespoons lukewarm water (80 to 85°F), divided
- 2 tablespoons plus 2 teaspoons honey, divided
- 1 tablespoon traditional dry yeast
- ½ cup flax seeds
- ¼ cup poppy seeds
- ¼ cup sesame seeds
- ¼ cup sunflower seeds (raw)
- 4 tablespoons vegetable oil, divided
- 3 cups stone-ground whole wheat flour
- 2 cups unbleached white wheat flour

(JIM BELL)

NOTE: PLEASE READ HELPFUL TIPS ON P. 201 BEFORE BEGINNING.

Stir together ¼ cup of the lukewarm water and 1 teaspoon of the honey and sprinkle the yeast on top. Do not stir. Set mixture aside for 5 to 10 minutes to activate yeast.

In a small bowl, combine flax seeds, poppy seeds, sesame seeds, and sunflower seeds. Set aside.

In large bowl, combine 2¼ cups of the lukewarm water, 3 tablespoons of the oil, and 2 tablespoons of the honey. Stir. Pour in softened yeast mixture and stir. Add the whole wheat flour. Using a wooden spoon, beat steadily and enthusiastically, until the strands of gluten are long and elastic. Add half the seed mix and 1½ cups of the white flour, continuing to beat as long as you can.

When you find the dough too difficult to mix with the spoon, turn it out onto a lightly floured surface and knead in remaining flour, adding only enough flour to keep the dough from sticking to your hands, until you have a pliable consistency—not too sticky, not too dry. Knead gently and rhythmically, but with strength, until the dough is smooth and elastic.

Clean the large bowl and oil with 1 tablespoon of the vegetable oil. Return the dough to the bowl, turning the dough to coat the surface. Cover bowl with a tea towel and place in a warm spot, allowing the dough to rise until doubled in size—roughly 2 hours or longer, depending on how warm your kitchen is.

When the dough has risen, gently press out the carbon dioxide with your fist and fold the dough over itself, turning it out onto a lightly floured counter. Divide into two even pieces. Knead each gently—a few strokes to free air pockets and bubbles—and shape into two round loaves.

Lightly grease a cookie sheet with vegetable oil. Roll each loaf in the remaining seed mix until entire loaves are coated. Place well apart on prepared cookie sheet. Beat the remaining 1 teaspoon honey into the remaining 2 tablespoons lukewarm water and glaze loaves with this wash to secure the seeds.

Cover with a tea towel and allow to rise again until just doubled in size—generally about half the time of the first rise.

Preheat oven to 400°F. Bake loaves for about 15 minutes, then reduce oven temperature to 375°F and continue to bake for about 35 minutes until loaves sound hollow when tapped on the bottom. If at any point the tops are browning too much, cover lightly with foil.

Cool on a wire rack or wooden breadboard.

> In the early days of the bakery, there was a store called Mary Jane's Alternative Tastes on Hollis Street in Halifax that I delivered bread to. A young woman working there as a shopkeeper asked me, "Have you ever made seed bread?" I said, "No. Tell me about it."
>
> She said, "Well, it's just a mixture of seeds in the bread. It's really tasty."
>
> "Wow. That's a good idea."
>
> The very next day I made a batch of seed bread. It's still, to this day, my favourite bread. – GAEL WATSON

Cheddar Cheese Scones

These scones are Gael's earliest baking memory.

MAKES 8 TO 12 SCONES

- 2 cups unbleached white flour
- 1 tablespoon baking powder
- 1 teaspoon salt
- ½ teaspoon freshly ground pepper
- ½ cup butter, cold
- 1 cup grated cheddar cheese
- 1 large egg yolk
- ¾ cup buttermilk (variations: cream, whole milk, or sour cream as 1:1 replacements)

(JIM BELL)

Preheat oven to 400°F. Lightly grease a cookie sheet with butter; alternatively, cover a cookie sheet with parchment.

Sift together flour, baking powder, salt, and pepper. Grate cold butter into dry mixture, then mix lightly with your fingertips. Add grated cheese and stir to combine.

In a separate bowl, mix together the egg yolk and buttermilk. Stir lightly into flour mixture. (Note: set this buttermilk-and-egg mixing bowl aside. There will be enough liquid left in the bowl to later brush onto the tops of the scones.)

Turn dough out onto lightly floured counter and knead gently, no more than three or four times, to bring together.

Roll into a round, ¾-inch–thick disc, then cut disc into 8 to 12 wedges, depending on the size you prefer. Place each wedge separately on cookie sheet. Brush the top of each scone with the leftover buttermilk and egg mixture from the bowl.

Bake for 10 to 12 minutes, until puffed up and golden.

My father taught me how to make scones when I was really young. They were the first thing I ever baked. I was six, maybe seven years old. And cheese scones. He would always say, "Just take whatever cheeses—bits and pieces—are left in the fridge. Use them all." So steeped in memory. My goodness, scones were just part of our life. They're the best. Split them, toast them, butter them. It's a quick bread. I love being able to suddenly produce something. "Quick, quick! Somebody's coming in the door." You just have to throw them together and throw them in a hot oven. – GAEL WATSON

Sweets Recipes

(Jim Bell)

Butter Tarts

MAKES 12 TO 14 TARTS

Pastry

- 2½ cups unbleached white flour
- 1 teaspoon salt
- 2 teaspoons sugar
- ½ pound butter, cold
- 2 egg yolks
- 2 tablespoons water, very cold

Filling

- 3¾ cups brown sugar
- 1½ teaspoons unbleached white wheat flour
- 1½ teaspoons salt
- 4 eggs
- ¼ pound butter, melted but not hot
- ¼ cup milk
- ¾ cup raisins
- ¾ cup chopped pecans or walnuts

(JIM BELL)

Preheat oven to 375°F. Prepare 12 to 14 paper muffin-cup liners by pressing each one out flat; set aside.

Prepare the pastry: sift together flour, salt, and sugar. Cut butter into small chunks and rub into flour mix with fingers until mixture is in pea-sized pieces. (Alternatively, grate cold butter into flour mix and lightly mix with your fingertips.)

Refrigerate mixture for 10 minutes to harden the butter. Remove from refrigerator, add egg yolks, and stir. Sprinkle in cold water and mix lightly. Form a ball and turn out onto a lightly floured counter. Press dough into a flat disc. Roll out to ¼-inch thickness. Cut pastry into circles a little larger than the muffin cups. Place each disc of pastry onto the flattened paper and ease each one into a standard muffin tin, pressing into the bottom and sides of each cup. Do not crimp the pastry.

Prepare the filling: place the brown sugar in a large bowl. Add flour and salt to the brown sugar and mix. Add eggs, one at a time, being careful not to overmix. (Note: do not beat the eggs beforehand; this will cause the sugar mixture to boil over in the oven.) Add melted butter and milk. Stir.

Place a generous quantity of raisins and/or nuts into each prepared pastry cup. Stir the filling to ensure that the brown sugar hasn't sunk to the bottom and add this filling to each cup until about three-quarters full.

Bake for 30 minutes, rotating the pan after 15 minutes. Tarts are done when filling is no longer jiggly.

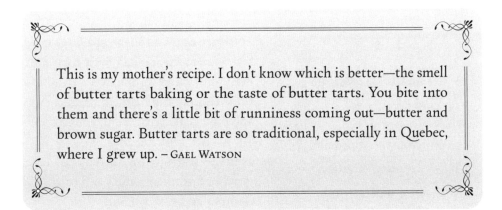

This is my mother's recipe. I don't know which is better—the smell of butter tarts baking or the taste of butter tarts. You bite into them and there's a little bit of runniness coming out—butter and brown sugar. Butter tarts are so traditional, especially in Quebec, where I grew up. – GAEL WATSON

Carrot Cake

MAKES ONE 13 X 9 X 2-INCH PAN OR ONE 12-CUP BUNDT PAN

Cake

- 1 cup unbleached white wheat flour
- 1 cup whole wheat flour
- 2 teaspoons baking soda
- 1 teaspoon baking powder
- 1 tablespoon cinnamon
- ½ teaspoon salt
- 3 eggs
- 2 cups sugar
- 1 cup sunflower or canola oil
- 1 teaspoon pure vanilla extract
- 4 medium carrots, grated
- 1 cup crushed pineapple, well drained
- 1 cup chopped walnuts (optional)
- 1 cup raisins (optional)

Cream Cheese Frosting

- ½ pound cream cheese, softened
- ½ pound butter, softened
- 1 teaspoon pure vanilla extract
- 5 cups icing sugar, sifted

(JIM BELL)

Preheat oven to 350°F. Using oil or butter, grease and flour a 13 x 9 x 2-inch baking pan or a 12-cup Bundt pan.

In a medium bowl, combine both flours, baking soda, baking powder, cinnamon, and salt.

Place eggs and sugar in a large bowl. Using an electric mixer, beat for 1 minute. Add oil and vanilla extract and mix until thoroughly blended. Add carrots and pineapple. Stir. Add dry ingredients all at once and mix, by hand or with a mixer, just until no streaks of flour remain. Sprinkle in nuts and raisins (if desired) and stir by hand.

Pour cake mixture into prepared pan. Bake for 55 to 60 minutes. Cake is done when a toothpick inserted in the centre comes out clean. Cool for 15 minutes before removing from pan.

When cake has cooled, prepare the frosting: using an electric mixer, beat together cream cheese, butter, and vanilla extract until fully blended. With mixer on low speed, slowly add icing sugar. Beat until frosting has a smooth, creamy consistency.

Spread evenly on cooled cake.

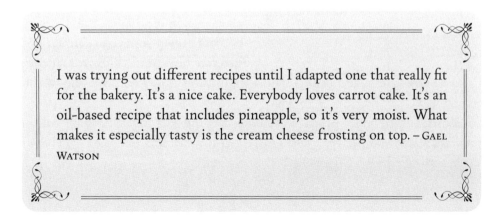

> I was trying out different recipes until I adapted one that really fit for the bakery. It's a nice cake. Everybody loves carrot cake. It's an oil-based recipe that includes pineapple, so it's very moist. What makes it especially tasty is the cream cheese frosting on top. – GAEL WATSON

Date Squares

MAKES ONE 8 X 8 X 2-INCH PAN

Date Filling

- ½ pound dates, chopped
- ½ cup cold water
- zest of ½ orange
- 2 tablespoons brown sugar
- 2 tablespoons orange juice
- 1 teaspoon fresh lemon juice

Base/Topping

- ½ cup unbleached white wheat flour
- ½ teaspoon baking soda
- 1 teaspoon baking powder
- ¼ teaspoon salt
- 1 cup butter, softened
- 1 cup brown sugar
- 1½ cups large flake rolled oats

(JIM BELL)

Preheat oven to 325°F. Lightly grease an 8 x 8 x 2–inch baking pan with vegetable oil.

Prepare the filling: in a small saucepan, combine dates, water, orange zest, and brown sugar and simmer over moderate heat until thick and smooth. Remove from heat; add orange and lemon juices and stir. Set aside to cool completely.

While filling cools, prepare the base/topping: sift together flour, baking soda, baking powder, and salt. Using an electric mixer, mix in butter. Add brown sugar and rolled oats. Mix well.

Spread half of the base/topping mixture in prepared baking pan. Pat to smooth. Spread the cooled date filling to evenly cover this base, then cover the filling with the remaining base/topping mixture.

Bake for 30 to 35 minutes. Increase heat to 350°F and bake for another 10 minutes, until golden. Cut into squares while hot and allow to cool in pan.

> I use my mother's date square recipe at the bakery—it's what I grew up with. There's nothing quite like a date square with a cup of hot tea on the side when you need a charge of energy at three o'clock in the afternoon. – GAEL WATSON

Lemon Squares

MAKES ONE 13 X 9 X 2-INCH PAN

Base
- 1 cup butter
- ½ cup sugar
- 2 cups unbleached white wheat flour

Topping
- ¼ cup unbleached flour
- 1 teaspoon baking powder
- 2 cups sugar
- 4 eggs
- ½ cup freshly squeezed lemon juice
- 1 cup shredded coconut

Lemon Frosting
- ½ pound butter, softened
- 1 tablespoon lemon zest
- ¼ cup freshly squeezed lemon juice
- 5 cups icing sugar, sifted

(JIM BELL)

Preheat oven to 350°F. Lightly grease a 13 x 9 x 2-inch baking pan with butter or vegetable oil.

Prepare base: mix butter, sugar, and flour by hand or with an electric mixer until crumbly. Press into prepared baking pan. Bake for 20 minutes.

While base bakes, prepare topping: combine flour, baking powder, sugar, eggs, and lemon juice. Blend with an electric mixer until well combined. Stir in coconut by hand.

226   LAHAVE BAKERY

When base has finished baking, remove from oven and pour topping over base. Return to 350°F oven and bake for 25 minutes. Allow to cool.

While squares cool, prepare the frosting: with an electric mixer, beat the butter, lemon zest, and lemon juice until fully blended. At a low speed, slowly add icing sugar and blend until smooth and creamy.

When pan has cooled, spread frosting on top and cut into squares.

> The lemon squares at the bakery are the most popular after the chocolate ones. They are smooth and creamy, with a buttery short-bread crust. – GAEL WATSON

Mocha Cake

MAKES ONE 13 X 9 X 2-INCH PAN

Wet Mixture

- ½ cup cocoa (German dark cocoa is ideal)
- ¼ cup instant coffee granules
- 1½ cups boiling water

Creamed Mixture

- ¾ cups butter
- 1¾ cups sugar
- 3 eggs
- 1 teaspoon vanilla extract

Dry Mixture

- 2 cups unbleached white wheat flour
- 2 teaspoons baking soda
- ½ teaspoon baking powder
- ½ teaspoon salt

Mocha Frosting

- 2 tablespoons instant coffee granules
- 2 tablespoons hot water
- 2 tablespoons dark cocoa (German dark cocoa is ideal)
- ½ pound butter, softened
- 2 tablespoons milk
- 5 cups icing sugar, sifted

(Jim Bell)

Preheat oven to 350°F. Line a 13 x 9 x 2-inch baking pan with parchment; alternatively, grease lightly with butter or vegetable oil and dust lightly with flour.

Prepare wet mixture: stir cocoa and instant coffee into boiling water. Allow to cool completely.

Prepare creamed mixture: in a stand mixer, cream butter, sugar, eggs, and vanilla extract at high speed until light and fluffy in texture—about five minutes.

Prepare dry mixture: in a medium bowl, sift all dry mixture ingredients together—flour, baking soda, baking powder, and salt.

While beating the creamed mixture at regular speed, add dry ingredients to creamed mixture (in fourths) alternately with wet mixture (in thirds), beginning and ending with flour mixture. Do not overbeat.

Bake for 30 to 40 minutes.

When cake is cooled, prepare frosting: dissolve instant coffee in hot water. Stir in cocoa, butter, and milk until fully combined. Using an electric mixer at a low speed, slowly add icing sugar and continue to mix until frosting is smooth, creamy, and glossy. If too stiff, add 1 teaspoon at a time of milk and blend until frosting has a spreadable texture.

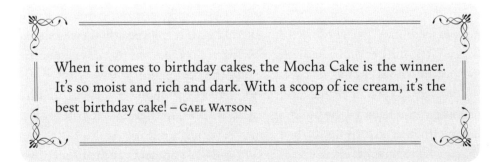

When it comes to birthday cakes, the Mocha Cake is the winner. It's so moist and rich and dark. With a scoop of ice cream, it's the best birthday cake! – GAEL WATSON

Acknowledgements

MANY PEOPLE CONTRIBUTED IN DIFFERENT WAYS TO MAKE THIS BOOK A REALITY. We thank them all sincerely for their time, for their contributions, for what they gave of themselves, shoring us up along the way. This book would not have been possible without them.

First and foremost, we wish to thank all nine participants whose interwoven voices tell the story of LaHave Bakery—especially Gael Watson, for entrusting us with bringing the story to life, for access to her voluminous archival materials, and for the privilege of accompanying her over many interviews as she revisited the highs and the lows of nearly four decades of the bakery's existence. Gloria Barrett, always larger than life, who provided candid and honest recollections at double-speed, punctuated throughout with uproarious laughter. Kathryn Gordon, who has been there from the very beginning, for thoughtfully and graciously sharing her memories. Peggy Greer, whom we affectionately came to refer to as "The Closer," for her eloquently succinct insights, making her a compelling witness to events in Gael's life. Bev Kaulback, for generously giving her personal inside view of what it's like to be an employee at LaHave Bakery. Laura Pitts, for her unbridled, free-flowing way of expressing herself, and for her behind-the-scenes look at what makes the business tick. Jesse Watson, for his particular view of the bakery through vivid childhood memories, and his ongoing connection to the building. Sadie Watson, for her unique perspective, having literally grown up in the bakery. Last but not least, Andra White, for sharing her astute observations of events and developments at the bakery over several decades, and for her genuine delight in being a part of it all.

We also wish to thank the following individuals: Anna Bald, for creating the painting showing the many components within the building, and for her beautiful artwork that has graced LaHave Bakery in many forms for many years; Marnie Troyer, creator of the iconic LaHave Bakery bread labels, for adapting her artwork for use in our book; the late Mary Troyer for her line drawing, from a c.1912 photograph, of the LaHave Outfitting Company building; Kat Frick Miller and Leslie Snidal for their amazing paintings; professional photographers Jim Bell and Peter Barss for their wonderful images; Stefan Porter for providing valuable feedback and context for the history chapter; Teresa MacKenzie, curator at the McCulloch House Museum and Genealogy Centre in Pictou, NS, for her help in tracing the old deeds to the property upon which the bakery now stands; Adrian Morrison, curator of collections at the Fisheries Museum of the Atlantic, Lunenburg, NS, for his help in tracking down supporting documents; Dianne Landry, Dalhousie University Archives assistant at the Killam Memorial Library in Halifax, NS, for giving access to hundreds of old records from the LaHave Outfitting Company; and, Ruth Seamone and Karen Fultz at the Fort Point Museum, LaHave, NS, for helping to fill in some gaps in the early history of the building.

We also wish to acknowledge Jane and Gael's brother, Leigh Robertson, for capturing in photographs the frightful condition of the LaHave Outfitters building just seven months before the bakery opened; and their beloved late sister, Kim Robertson Moss, an accomplished baker herself, for scaling down some of the LaHave Bakery sweets recipes for the book. We are indebted to our dear friends Eve Rosenberg and Mariah Irons for nourishing us with delicious meals, and for their ongoing loving support. Heartfelt thanks go to our longtime friends Trudy Watts and Ron Kelly, whom we entrusted with reading the manuscript, for their invaluable comments and suggestions, not to mention catching some of those ever-elusive typos. Sincere appreciation to Don Sedgwick for his helpful suggestions and advice as we neared the finish line.

To the many others who encouraged us along the way, we are grateful to each and every one of you.

Last, and importantly, we wish to thank Angela Mombourquette, our editor at Nimbus Publishing, for guiding us through every step of the process toward publication. A skilled communicator, we could always count on Angela to respond to any of our questions or concerns with amazing promptness. Her respectful, gentle approach to editing our work felt totally collaborative, and stayed true to the voices in the book. Who could ask for more?

Endnotes

1 Balcom, B. A., *History of the Lunenburg Fishing Industry*, (Lunenburg: Lunenburg Marine Museum Society, 1977), 30.

2 Ibid., 30

3 Ibid., 28.

4 Ibid., 28.

5 Ibid., 26.

6 "Big Catch of LaHave Fleet," Unknown newspaper, September 26, 1909.

7 "Hailings of LaHave Fishing Fleet Season 1917," *Bridgewater Bulletin*, February 16, 1972.

8 Balcom, *History of Lunenburg Fishing*, 6.

9 "Salt Cod, Chicken, Slavery and Yams," El Valle de Anton, Panama (blog) 2014, accessed November 10, 2021. elvalleinformation.wordpress.com/salt-cod-slavery/.

10 Ibid.

11 Prime, G., "Salt in Nova Scotia, 1991," Nova Scotia Department of Natural Resources, accessed January 18, 2022. novascotia.ca/natr/meb/data/pubs/ic/ic19.pdf.

12 Balcom, *History of Lunenburg Fishing*, 30.

13 "Lunenburg's Fishing Industry, 1870s–1940s," Historical Marker Database (HMDB) 2016, accessed March 20, 2022. hmdb.org/m.asp?m=78207.

14 Balcom, *History of Lunenburg Fishing*, 28.

15 "Town and Country News," *Bridgewater Bulletin*, March 5, 1901.

16 Gray, F., "Recalls Early Days of LaHave Outfitting Company," *Bridgewater Bulletin*, September 22, 1954.

17 "A New Fish Concern," *Bridgewater Bulletin*, September 12, 1905.

18 "The Atlantic Fish Companies Ltd: Combining and Comprising," *The Maritime Merchant*, July 12, 1906, 63.

19 "LaHave Couple to Mark 50th Anniversary Today," *Chronicle Herald*, February 8, 1949.

20 "Steamship *Portland*," Stellwagen Bank National Marine Sanctuary 2019, accessed March 24, 2022. stellwagen.noaa.gov/maritime/portland.html.

21 Cooke, R. K., "LaHave Mariner Spry at 84," *Bridgewater Bulletin*, 1958.

22 "Fire Destruction Amounts to $50,000 In West LaHave," *Bridgewater Bulletin*, August 22, 1923.

23 Cooke, "LaHave Mariner."

24 Gray, "Recalls Early Days."

25 "LaHave Cold Storage Plant," *Bridgewater Bulletin*, August 21, 1935.

26 "The Beam Trawler *Jutland*," *Saltwire*, 2017, accessed February 17, 2022. saltwire.com/atlantic-canada/business/the-beam-trawler-jutland-85595/.

27 Edwards, D., "The Prohibition Era & Rum Running," *Fairview Historical Society Articles Archives*, 2021, accessed April 20, 2023. fairviewhistoricalsociety.ca/the-prohibition-era-and-rum-running/.

28 Ibid.